The

HEAL YOUR

OCD

WORKBOOK

Text © 2009 John B. Arden, Ph.D., and Daniel DalCorso, Psy.D.

First published in the USA in 2009 by
Fair Winds Press, a member of
Quayside Publishing Group
100 Cummings Center
Suite 406-L
Beverly, MA 01915-6101
www.fairwindspress.com

12 11 10 09 08   1 2 3 4 5

ISBN-13: 978-1-59233-378-3
ISBN-10: 1-59233-378-8

Library of Congress Cataloging-in-Publication Data
Arden, John Boghosian.
  The heal-your-OCD workbook : new techniques for managing obsessive-com-
pulsive behaviors to improve your daily life and take back your peace of mind /
John B. Arden, Daniel DalCorso.
      p. cm.
   ISBN-13: 978-1-59233-378-3
   ISBN-10: 1-59233-378-8
   1. Obsessive-compulsive disorder—Popular works. I. DalCorso, Daniel. II.
Title.
   RC533.A754 2009
   616.85'227—dc22
                              2008052252

Cover design by everlution design
Book design by boston page pro

Printed and bound in China

*The information in this book is for educational purposes only. It is not intended to
replace the advice of a physician or medical practitioner. Please see your health care
provider before beginning any new health program.*

The HEAL YOUR 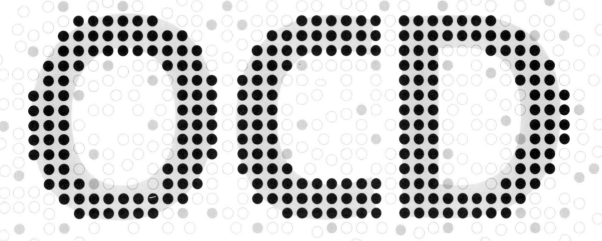 WORKBOOK

New Techniques to Improve Your Daily Life and Take Back Your Peace of Mind

John Arden, Ph.D.,
author of *Conquering Post-Traumatic Stress Disorder* and *The Heal Your Anxiety Workbook*
and Daniel Dal Corso, Psy.D.

FAIR WINDS
PRESS
BEVERLY, MASSACHUSETTS

Contents

Chapter 1
OCD Is Treatable!

Jonathan, a forty-one-year-old carpenter, loved running ever since competing on his high school track team. Now, however, he jogged thirty minutes each morning because he knew exercise was one of the best ways to keep his anxiety in check. After a good workout, his day generally went much smoother. But one autumn morning he noticed something on the road in front of a neighbor's house just a block from his own home. The lawn was covered with dried fallen leaves and on the street where he was running there was a small patch of broken glass. A few steps past the glass Jonathan stopped. He was sure he had stepped on the glass. He quickly became certain that as he ran over the glass his shoe had kicked a shard into the leaves on his neighbor's lawn. In the space of a few seconds, Jonathan constructed a frightening scenario that he couldn't get out of his mind. He imagined the sun shining through that shard, being focused and magnified until the leaves caught on fire. The fire spread, catching his own home on fire, killing his children.

Although Jonathan knew that scenario was highly improbable, he spent the next half hour searching his neighbor's lawn for a piece of glass that wasn't there. He was *obsessed* with thoughts of danger and *compelled* to take action in order to reduce his fear. These types of intrusive and frightening thoughts were daily occurrences for Jonathan. He spent most of the day fighting against his compulsions to protect himself and others from highly implausible dangers that existed only in his imagination. His thoughts and actions seriously impacted his relationships with his wife and children. His wife was the only person he confided in until the problem became so severe that she insisted he seek professional help.

Obsessive-compulsive disorder (OCD for short) is a form of anxiety that comes in a variety of types and intensities. It is defined by repeated, intrusive, unwanted thoughts, called obsessions, often (but not always) about frightening things that are very hard to get out of one's mind. These thoughts are followed by actions—either physical or mental—that are intended to reduce the uncomfortable, anxious feelings. These are called compulsions because people feel compelled to do them to relieve their anxiety.

Most people with OCD don't know what it is or that they have it. To make matters worse, many health care professionals are not trained to ask the right questions that will lead to diagnosis and treatment. To compound the problem even further, people with OCD are usually so confused or embarrassed by their symptoms that they don't tell anyone. This all adds up to a lot of unnecessary suffering.

If you think you might have OCD, there are three very important things you need to know right away. The first is that OCD is highly treatable! Let that sink in for a second or two. Yes, OCD is treatable with or without medication. This means that you really can feel better than you do today. If you're like a lot of people with OCD, you may have given up on feeling better or worry that you'll have these same problems for the rest of your life. Second, some people are even afraid that because they have OCD it means they're crazy. That's just plain wrong! *People with OCD are not crazy.* OCD is highly treatable.

Rewire Your Brain and Feel Better

Third, you need to understand that getting better comes down to rewiring a part of your brain that only learns by doing. That's why the exercises in this book can be more effective than taking medicine to control your OCD. (We'll talk more about medications for OCD later because there are definite pros and cons to taking them.) But like reprogramming a computer, you need to know something about how your brain works in order to undo the part that doesn't work. And we're here to guide you in properly installing new and better instructions. Just remember, small steps lead to big results. As with programming a computer, it needs to be done in the right sequence. But don't worry, we'll lead you through the process step by step, and before long you'll start seeing your progress because you'll notice that you feel less anxious and more in control.

The First Thing to Do

Okay, let's get started with something simple that will begin building your repertoire of habits that will help you feel better. Simply stop for a few seconds and notice how anxious or uncomfortable you're feeling right now. What is your present state of comfort or discomfort?

Anxiety is measured in what are referred to as SUDs, which stands for "subjective units of discomfort." On a scale of 1 to 100, how anxious or uncomfortable are you? Imagine that "100" means you're jumping out of your skin, you feel as if you can't take it another second, and "1" means you're relaxed, as if you've just woken up from the most delicious sleep imaginable. Assess how you're feeling at this moment and rate it 1 to 100.

Later, when you get into your individualized treatment program, we'll ask you to make a habit of recording your SUD score. But for now, just noticing and coming up with a number to measure your discomfort is enough. This sounds easy to do, and it is. But many people with anxiety in general and OCD in particular don't want to reflect on their level of discomfort. On the one hand, it's natural to try to avoid something that might make us uncomfortable. On the other hand, however, avoiding things can make a problem bigger than it is. This is what happens with OCD.

Knowing what you are feeling is the beginning of your treatment. This ability is called "interoception," meaning to feel your body's inner sensations. It's important to know the reality of your anxiety rather than what you think it might be. Many people feel that they're at a 100 all the time, and when they start paying attention and recording their actual SUD scores they find things aren't nearly as bad as they thought. We all tend to remember the bad things more easily than the good. We'll return to the subject of SUD scores later with more instructions on how to use them to measure your progress. But if you haven't done so already:

1. Stop reading.
2. Close your eyes for a few seconds.
3. Sense how your body is feeling.
4. Rate your anxiety/discomfort from 1 to 100.

Excellent! You just began your treatment program.

How This Book Can Help You

You'll learn what OCD is and how you can treat yourself with a powerful treatment technique called "exposure with response prevention." We'll explain why this treatment works and teach you how to use it. You will learn which behaviors lead to success, as we share with you examples of treatment plans for problems similar to yours.

We'll lead you through a series of written exercises that will help you design a treatment plan that's customized to your needs. You'll be able to target what you most want to work on, at the pace you're comfortable with. By following the exercises described in this book, you will create a systematic, step-by-step series of activities that have a good likelihood of leading you to a life of substantially reduced OCD symptoms.

What you need to bring to this is the willingness to invest the time and energy to read and do the recommended exercises. Once you've developed your individualized treatment plan, you'll need the commitment to follow through. You probably can't make that commitment right now because you don't know what your treatment plan includes. But you *can* commit to reading this book and developing your treatment plan.

We encourage you not to suffer any longer than you need to. The sooner you begin, the sooner you'll experience symptom relief. Although your relief is unlikely to be 100 percent, it could well be substantial enough to dramatically improve your life. And with perseverance, you can begin to experience this kind of improvement in a matter of weeks.

Chapter 2

What Is OCD . . . and Do I Have It?

What Is OCD?

OCD is a form of anxiety that involves unwanted, intrusive thoughts that can range from annoying to frightening to repulsive, and even disturbingly bizarre. Because these thoughts are so difficult to get out of one's mind they are called "obsessive" thoughts. At their core, obsessive thoughts often involve relatively normal concerns, reactions, worries, and fears that get blown out of proportion. An obsessing person loses track of the real-world likelihood of his or her thoughts coming true. Typically, the more one resists such thoughts, the stronger and more uncomfortable they become. Because obsessive thoughts are not easily dismissed, a person besieged by them cannot readily follow the advice of family and friends to "just think about something else."

Common topics that trigger obsessive thoughts are:

- Cleanliness, germs, contamination
- Safety, security
- Perfection, correctness, orderliness, exactness
- Need to save or collect things
- Aggression, violence
- Immorality, sexuality, perversity

These are subjects that everyone thinks about, hears and reads about, has been taught about, or has some personal experience with. Many require us to make daily decisions to ensure our health and safety. Others are less common. OCD, however, is an anxious response that is far more easily triggered, is vastly more intense, and lasts much longer than "normal" concerns. As we'll discuss in more detail later, these thoughts activate the brain and body's anxiety response. The reason anxiety is so uncomfortable is that it's our brain's way of getting us to do something to stop the feeling. It motivates us and focuses our attention on fixing the problem.

Actions taken to stop obsessive thoughts are referred to as "compulsions" or "rituals" because the person feels *compelled* to carry them out to neutralize the thoughts and reduce the accompanying anxious feelings. Compulsions can be thoughts as well as behaviors. The word *ritual* suggests a specific technique or sequence, a "correct" way of performing the compulsion, a fixed, inflexible pattern that the person believes is necessary for anxiety reduction. Compulsions are generally understood to be excessive even by the person doing them.

Common compulsions include excessive:

- Hand washing, bathing, grooming, housecleaning
- Avoiding "contaminated" objects
- Checking doors, windows, locks, stoves, other appliances
- Counting, praying, repeating words
- Retracing your movements or driving route to ensure that you didn't inadvertently hurt someone on the way
- Collecting, saving, stockpiling, hoarding

Compulsive behaviors are often related in a logical way to obsessive thoughts. That is, a person with an obsessive fear of germs or contamination may have hand washing and housecleaning compulsions. Obsessive thoughts about safety may be followed by compulsive checking of locks on the doors and windows. Obsessive thoughts about immoral behavior may be followed by compulsive prayer. However, sometimes there is no logical link between the obsession and the compulsion. This seems especially true with the compulsion to count things or repeat words or phrases until there is a sense of things being in order or feeling "just right."

One interesting characteristic of OCD that has been noted by some clinicians is that the worry or fear is frequently for the safety of others. For example, OCD sometimes first develops in women soon after having a child. Their obsessive thoughts revolve around the safety of their child. Of course, it's normal for a mother to be concerned for her child's safety. As most mothers (and fathers), especially those with young children, would agree, there is a near-constant thought process about where your children are; whether they are properly dressed, fed, or covered up; whether they have sunscreen on; whether their homework is done; whether they are eating too much sugar; and on and on. The difference, as we mentioned, has to do with how easily and frequently those fears get triggered, how uncomfortable they make you, how long the thoughts persist, and what you need to do to calm yourself.

Although compulsions seem to reduce anxiety in the moment and help you calm down, they are actually what keep OCD brain circuits activated and strong. The more you engage in a ritual, the stronger the brain circuits supporting this habit become. In the section on treatment, we'll discuss in detail how you can make use of this knowledge to weaken your OCD brain circuits while simultaneously strengthening healthier alternative circuits.

Do I Have OCD?

There is a wide range of OCD symptom intensity. Some people have such severe OCD that they spend many hours each day completely dominated by it. Other people have milder symptoms that don't require a lot of time and are easily hidden, even from people close to them. Not everyone who suffers from obsessions and compulsions would qualify for an "official" diagnosis of OCD. However, if you can relate to the kinds of thoughts and behaviors described in this section, then this book is for you.

Let's look at examples of the different types of OCD so you can identify which one or ones affect you. Often people who suffer from OCD have more than one form of it.

The main categories of compulsive behaviors are:

- Washing and cleaning
- Checking
- Repeating
- Counting
- Needing order and perfection
- Hoarding
- Engaging in thought rituals

Because behaviors are more easily categorized than thoughts, OCD is classified by the type of compulsion or ritualistic behavior used to diminish anxiety or discomfort. An exception to this is the "thought rituals" type, because there is no overt repeated behavior used to attempt to alleviate the anxiety. In this case, the repeated compulsive behaviors are all done mentally. Let's look at these types of OCD one at a time.

Washing and Cleaning

People with this form of OCD have a keen sense of where germs may be hiding and/or a heightened sensitivity to "contamination." It's not uncommon for people with this form of OCD to avoid shaking hands with others, and they may have developed clever ways in and out of public buildings to avoid the need to touch a door handle. Touching money is another frequent concern.

People with washing and cleaning compulsions often wash their hands, arms, or entire bodies after touching or believing they were contaminated by something.

Housecleaning rituals are also common, particularly among women, with this type of OCD. This often includes frequent vacuuming and excessive cleaning of the kitchen or bathrooms. Obsessive cleaners often frequently downplay this at first, just saying they like their home to be orderly.

Checking

Some people check things repeatedly to make sure that they, their family members, and others they came in contact with are safe. Stoves, irons, and locks on doors and windows are the most commonly checked objects. You might be thinking of course these things need to be checked. One difference between "normal" and OCD checking is that typically once is not enough. OCD often compels people to check three or more times before they're satisfied that things are secure. During the course of checking, people frequently have the sense that they are checking more than they need to but they just can't stop until they have done it the way that gives them a feeling of certainty.

Another common checking activity is retracing one's movements or driving route to ensure that no one has been harmed. Some people will watch the news to verify that they didn't cause harm, accidents, or a catastrophe during the course of their daily activities. Others will inspect their bodies to ensure no injuries or diseases are evident and may frequently visit the doctor or ask family members for reassurance that they are okay. Repeatedly asking for reassurance is a common behavior for "checkers" as well as people with other types of OCD.

Repeating

Repeating involves behaviors that are done multiple times, typically until the person feels that the action was done "just right." These behaviors are generally associated with reducing a sense of discomfort rather than fear. Commonly repeated activities include dressing and undressing, buttoning and unbuttoning clothing, stepping in and out of a room, opening and closing doors or cabinets, reading or writing things down several times, doing routine activities "the right number of times," such as turning light switches on and off repeatedly.

Counting

People with counting compulsions often regard certain numbers as good or bad. Objects or thoughts that involve bad numbers need to be reorganized or redone to include good ones. Odd or even numbers might represent good or bad luck, and the number of coins in one's pocket or bills in the wallet, or the number of steps or breaths taken, may need to be counted in sets of good numbers. Good numbers can be different for different activities. Some people with washing compulsions feel the need to wash the "correct" number of times.

Needing Order and Perfection

People with an obsessive-compulsive need for order or perfection often find themselves taking longer with tasks than others do. They might be slowed by a need to verify accuracy of contents, spelling, or computations. When the emphasis is on order, there may be a need to align objects exactly, such as a stack of papers, the placement of furniture, clothing in a closet, knickknacks on a shelf, or mirrors or pictures on the wall. As with other types of OCD, this may take a few extra seconds or be so overwhelming that people have trouble leaving their homes because things need to be perfect.

Hoarding

Hoarders keep things that other people would throw away with little deliberation. Frequently hoarded objects include newspapers, magazines, articles clipped from print material, jars, cans, bags, clothes, boxes, empty food containers, and nails and other building supplies. It is not uncommon to hear about people living in homes that are so packed with things that there are only paths through the stuff in each room, no open space. Often they believe that these objects are valuable, will be read or utilized later, or will be needed at some point in the future.

Engaging in Thought Rituals

Thought rituals often are triggered by intrusive thoughts or images a person may have of harm, disaster, aggression, violence, sexual acts, or other immoral or blasphemous behavior committed by them. The thought ritual, then, is the mental act intended to undo or neutralize the previous thought so as to avoid such thoughts actually causing harm. Thought rituals can take many forms, including prayer, asking forgiveness, striking a bargain with God, mentally saying the opposite of the dangerous thought, thinking a "magical" phrase a set number of times, or imagining the "disaster scenario" turning out satisfactorily.

If I Do These Things, Doesn't It Mean I'm Crazy?

Although OCD thoughts and behaviors can be odd, frightening, and even downright bizarre, it DOES NOT mean you are crazy. This fear has probably prevented more people from getting help than any other misconception about OCD—don't let it stop you. Take encouragement from the treatment successes of others like you.

OCD is by no means rare—two or three people out of a hundred suffer from it. You probably know a hundred people (between family, workplace, neighbors, church or synagogue, etc.). It is highly likely that in that group of people there are one or two who also have OCD. You are not alone. Unfortunately, people with OCD are very good at hiding the fact due to shame and embarrassment.

As the study of mental disorders advances, the list of what was once considered "crazy" grows smaller each year. The words *crazy* (not a legal or professional term) and *insane* (a legal term) are frequently used by laypeople to mean all kinds of things. Professionally, there is a very narrow band of disorders called psychoses that are characterized by being out of touch with reality. In psychotic states people cannot distinguish their thoughts from reality. And even these kinds of disorders can be controlled somewhat with medications.

This is different from OCD. Most adults with OCD know that their thoughts and behaviors are odd. They would prefer not to have obsessive thoughts or engage in compulsions but are at a loss as to how to control them. (This is not the case for children with

OCD. They usually accept their thoughts and behaviors as normal.) During severe obsessive thoughts, people may be convinced that their fears are true. But in a calmer moment they know that they overreacted and would choose a different way of being if they knew how.

There is no reason for people with OCD to continue to suffer. The fear of "officially" being labeled "crazy" has prevented far too many people from seeking help. If you have been afraid to get help, you have made a good start by reading this far. Your greatest ally in getting healthier is to know as much as you need to about OCD and then take action to change it. (But don't let yourself get lost in an endless search for information and use that as an excuse to delay helping yourself.)

After reading and responding to the next section you'll be in a better position to know whether to continue with the self-help portion of this book, seek help from a mental health professional, or do both. Remember, knowledge is power, but active treatment is required to get your OCD under control.

Shame and Embarrassment

People suffering from anxiety are generally prone to avoid getting help for what bothers them because anxiety is their normal internal state. And because anxiety generates thoughts about how to protect yourself and others from potential threats, it's often difficult to distinguish between normal and abnormal anxiety.

People suffering from OCD are often very ashamed and embarrassed because their thoughts and behaviors are quite unusual. It's not uncommon for people to have grappled with OCD for many years before seeking help. In our experience, OCD is most often uncovered in a diagnostic interview when a person comes in for therapy for another problem, such as anxiety. That is, OCD is revealed during the process of asking questions and probing deeper into what a person says. Rarely does anyone volunteer information about their odd thoughts or behav-iors, though once the topic is broached they are generally relieved to be talking with a clinician who understands. Most people who have OCD have wondered whether they have it, or know they have it, yet don't offer that infor-mation until asked about it directly.

It is sad but true; medical doctors are likely to miss this diagnosis. For one, they are not looking for it because they're not trained to. They are looking for physical causes for problems. Compound that with the reluctance on the part of an OCD sufferer to talk about it and a person can go for years without getting properly diagnosed. A medical doctor may detect the presence of anxiety but not be aware of the specific form of anxiety. Suggestion: Tell your health care providers, "I have OCD. Can you help me?"

If the descriptions and examples in the previous chapter sound all too familiar, it's time to find out more about the type(s) of OCD that impact you. Let's take an inventory. We'll start with compulsive behaviors because, in most cases, they are more overt. Then we'll help you inventory your obsessions. Remember that compulsions are behaviors or mental acts you feel driven to perform and feel noticeably anxious or uncomfortable if you're unable to.

Put a checkmark next to each type of compulsion you engage in. Check as many that apply. People with OCD will often mark several areas. At the end of the list for each type of compulsion, jot down other similar behaviors that you do, even if you aren't 100 percent certain that they are compulsions. This will help you assess the extent of your own OCD affliction.

Washing and Cleaning

The list below includes common things that OCD sufferers overwash or overclean, often in ritualistic ways. If your frequency and intensity of cleaning and washing the following items is well within the range of normal, don't check it. However, if you know or suspect you're doing more than most other people, mark that item.

I feel compelled to wash or clean:

- ❑ My hands
- ❑ My entire body
- ❑ Kitchen counters and floors
- ❑ Dishes, utensils
- ❑ Clothes, shoes
- ❑ Carpets, rugs
- ❑ The bathroom
- ❑ Closets
- ❑ Computer keyboards, phones
- ❑ My car
- ❑ The garage
- ❑ The yard
- ❑ The driveway
- ❑ Other (specify) _____

A close cousin to excessive cleaning and washing is avoiding things that would trigger the need to do so. Review the following list and see whether any of these relate to your overcleaning impulses.

I feel compelled to avoid things because I fear contamination from:

- ❑ Germs, dirt, dust, grease
- ❑ Doorknobs, handles
- ❑ Shaking hands with or touching others
- ❑ Food, especially raw meat
- ❑ Public restrooms
- ❑ Money
- ❑ Blood, feces, urine, saliva, sweat
- ❑ Animal fur
- ❑ Hair
- ❑ Gas pumps

- ❑ Certain people or races of people
- ❑ Neighborhoods, buildings, parts of town
- ❑ Other (specify) _____

Checking

I feel compelled to check:

- ❑ Doors and windows are shut or locked
- ❑ Appliances such as stoves or irons are off or unplugged
- ❑ Refrigerator door is closed
- ❑ Faucets are off
- ❑ Paperwork is complete and/or accurate
- ❑ News sources to see whether I caused an accident or hurt someone without knowing it
- ❑ My blood pressure, blood sugar, pulse, temperature
- ❑ My driving route or other action to see whether I harmed someone without knowing it
- ❑ Food (for hidden objects such as insect parts or poisons)
- ❑ My body, looking for signs of illness or injury
- ❑ List other things you check _____
  _____
  _____
  _____

Repeating

I feel compelled to do things a certain number of times or until I feel "just right" or complete:

- ❑ Saying (aloud or silently) words, phrases, prayers, songs
- ❑ Humming, throat clearing, special noises
- ❑ Turning lights on and off
- ❑ Walking in and out of doors
- ❑ Zipping, buttoning, dressing
- ❑ Reading words, sentences, etc.
- ❑ Touching, knocking, tapping, rubbing something a specific number of times
- ❑ Asking for reassurance
- ❑ Other (specify) _____

Counting

I feel compelled to count:

- ❑ Words
- ❑ Steps
- ❑ Breaths
- ❑ Touches, taps, knocks
- ❑ Sounds
- ❑ Objects in pocket, purse, wallet
- ❑ Thoughts (number of times a word, phrase, or object occurs)
- ❑ People, cars, objects passed
- ❑ Types of things such as type of garment, make of car, or brand of beverage
- ❑ Random objects
- ❑ Ceiling tiles
- ❑ Other (specify) _____

Needing Order and Perfection

I feel compelled to:

- ❑ Straighten, align, smooth, or level things
- ❑ Order things (put them in "proper" sequence)
- ❑ Arrange things (into a pattern that feels "just right")
- ❑ Pick up/clean/remove things that interfere with perfection
- ❑ Other (specify) _____

Hoarding

I feel compelled to collect and/or am uncomfortable divesting myself of:

- ❑ Newspapers, magazines, articles
- ❑ Jars, bottles, cans
- ❑ Clothing, shoes
- ❑ String, rubber bands
- ❑ Tools, building materials, scraps
- ❑ Cars, lawnmowers, engine parts
- ❑ Stuffed animals, dolls
- ❑ Things I find on the street
- ❑ Other (specify) _____

Engaging in Thought Rituals

I feel compelled to "fix" things by using mental actions, such as:

- ❑ Praying
- ❑ Repeating certain words or phrases silently

- ❑ Undoing a thought by thinking its opposite
- ❑ Asking friends and family for reassurance
- ❑ Other mental ritual _____

I can't stop thinking about things I have done, might have done, or might do:

- ❑ Mistakes, embarrassments
- ❑ Something said during the day
- ❑ Sex—I'm afraid that I might do things such as molest a child, rape someone, ask someone to have sex, or become homosexual
- ❑ Accidentally hurt myself, loved ones, strangers
- ❑ Violence—I'm afraid that against my will, I might hurt myself, loved ones, strangers
- ❑ I might cause catastrophic accidents
- ❑ I may cause other harm by my thoughts
- ❑ Sinful or blasphemous acts
- ❑ Other (specify) _____

It's important that you have a good inventory of your compulsions. Go back over the above lists and make sure you checked everything that applies to you. Be sure to include compulsions (or "pure obsessions"—obsessions that are not followed by an obvious compulsive behavior) that aren't in our list. List things even if you're not 100 percent sure. Go over your behaviors with a fine-tooth comb and make this list as exhaustive as possible. Do not read on until you've completed the above.

Now estimate the average amount of time spent per day on each type of compulsive behavior and the obsessive thoughts that trigger your anxiety or discomfort. Jot down those estimates in the chart below. Then total those amounts and write that in the bottom row. You're only estimating the amount of time you spend, so you don't need to be exact. You just want to figure out whether you're spending minutes or hours. And if it's hours, approximately how many? If you feel like you're taking a wild guess, that's fine, but take the best wild guess you can. Then over the next few days you can monitor yourself to see whether your guess was about right or needs to be adjusted. This estimate will help you determine the severity of your symptoms.

Once you've completed the chart below, you can interpret your symptom severity level using the measures on the next page.

Compulsions and Obsessions Time Chart

	TIME SPENT ON COMPULSIONS	TIME SPENT ON OBSESSIONS
Washing and Cleaning		
Checking		
Repeating		
Counting		
Needing Order and Perfection		
Hoarding		
Engaging in Thought Rituals		
Total Time		

Symptom Severity Chart

SYMPTOM SEVERITY	TOTAL TIME SPENT	EFFECT ON DAILY FUNCTIONING
Mild	Less than 1 hour	Slight interference with social or occupational function
Moderate	1 to 2 hours	Noticeable interference with daily functioning
Moderately severe	2 to 3 hours	Substantial impairment
Severe	3 to 8 hours	Very substantial impairment
Very severe	More than 8 hours	Incapacitating

This assessment of your symptoms and their impact on your life will help you make the right decisions about the treatment recommendations in the following chapter. You're now ready to make those decisions and chart your route away from OCD.

Chapter 3

Treatment Options, Obstacles, and Readiness

This chapter will explain the different types of treatment that are available for OCD and the things you need to bear in mind when choosing the one that's right for you, based on the severity of your symptoms. Then we'll explain some frequently encountered obstacles and common problems that coexist with OCD. At that point, you'll have an opportunity to assess your readiness to proceed and the strengths and weaknesses you bring to treatment. After reading this chapter, you might discuss it with a close family member or friend to help you decide which option to take.

Treatment Options

You have several options for treatment. These can be done individually or in combination with one another. Each option has pros and cons. It's important to decide what's best for you. You deserve to be as close to symptom-free as possible. How you attain that depends on several factors. Personal preference plays a big role, but the realities of health insurance coverage, cost of private care, and factors such as fear, shame, and embarrassment all need to be considered. There are three main options. The third of these can be a supplement to the other two or the sole method. The three main categories of treatment are:

- **Manage symptoms with medication**
- **Work with a psychotherapist**
- **Self-help therapy**

You might make use of these options at different points in time. For instance, you might start with self-help and see whether you make the kind of progress you want. If so, great! If not, then you might decide you need the additional support of a psychotherapist to tackle your most difficult issues. Or you might start with medication, then find a psychotherapist to work with, and then utilize self-help to further extend your treatment gains. We'll give you some guidelines on how to choose among the options.

The most important thing, however, is that you begin some form of treatment and feel better as soon as possible. You may remember the first of the "three important things" we stated in this book: "OCD is highly treatable!" That statement is true, but only if you do things such as the exercises in this workbook. Although we would love for you to continue through our self-help recommendations and attain results that you cannot even imagine at this moment, the critical thing is to select the treatment that best fits your life circumstances. This section will help you consider your options so you can proceed with confidence.

To Medicate or Not to Medicate?

Some people prefer to control OCD with medication, others prefer no medication, and others are willing to do "whatever it takes." This decision should be based on the severity of your symptoms. (Remember our definition earlier: "Severe" means that your OCD occupies more than two hours per day and causes significant impairment in your ability to attend to daily responsibilities.) Medication can be highly effective in reducing OCD symptoms. Specifically, the class of medications typically referred to as antidepressants can be quite helpful. In fact, if your symptoms are severe, or you are also depressed, it's recommended that you take medication in addition to psychotherapy or self-help therapy.

Effective medications include the following brand names and their much less expensive generic counterparts in parentheses: Prozac (fluoxetine), Paxil (paroxetine), Zoloft (sertraline), Celexa (citalopram), Lexapro (escitalopram), Anafranil (clomipramine), and Luvox (fluvoxamine).

These medications act by increasing the availability of one of the brain's neurotransmitters: serotonin. Collectively, these medications are called "serotonin reuptake inhibitors," or "SRIs" for short. SRIs make serotonin work more efficiently in the brain. Increasing serotonin's ability to perform its function well can help people with many types of anxiety disorders, including OCD, as well as those with the very common mood problem of depression.

SRIs generally take four to six weeks to achieve a noticeable degree of OCD symptom control and in some cases take as long as eight to twelve weeks.

(Depressive symptoms, if present, are likely to begin to moderate within three or four weeks.) If you've been living with OCD for years and are fearful of engaging in the exercises described in this workbook and/or psychotherapy, medication could be a good option for you. It would be best to speak with a psychiatrist (a medical doctor specializing in mental health) for specific recommendations. Although primary care doctors can also prescribe SRIs, they are generally much less knowledgeable about OCD and therefore not as aggressive as a psychiatrist would be in treating it.

The SRIs, like most medications, do have some possible side effects, which include nausea, dizziness, drowsiness, headache, teeth clenching, vivid and strange dreams, changes in appetite, weight loss or gain, photo- sensitivity, and difficulty reaching orgasm in women and maintaining an erection in men. You may want to discuss these possibilities with your psychiatrist or physician.

The problem with using medication to control OCD, however, is that it does not make permanent changes in the brain. Although an SRI can be effective in relieving symptoms, it will only do so as long as you take it. Many people are willing to take medication indefinitely in exchange for getting OCD under control. Others use the symptom reduction they experience through medication to give them greater ability to engage in exposure with response prevention therapy (ERP), which is described in this book. Good, long-lasting results can be obtained by combining pharmacotherapy with ERP.

To use or not to use medication is a highly individual decision. There is no right or wrong. It depends on the severity of your symptoms and your willingness to tolerate discomfort (and there will be some with ERP, as we will explain later).

Working with a Psychotherapist

This is an excellent choice for anyone with OCD, provided you find a *cognitive-behavioral therapist* experienced with ERP. This will help you achieve your goal of OCD symptom reduction, reprogram your brain for lasting results, and provide support and encouragement through the process. Research has shown that ERP is the only therapy that's been consistently demonstrated to be effective with OCD. The results of ERP also hold up over time, and people who continue to make use of these principles get better and better. This type of therapy generally also includes elements of *cognitive therapy*, meaning a focus on reducing the distorted thoughts that accompany obsessions. If your OCD symptoms are severe (as defined earlier), we encourage you to invest your time, effort, and money in finding a therapist experienced in OCD treatment.

If you choose to pursue this option, remember that you will need to find a therapist who has an expertise in treating OCD and is trained in cognitive-behavioral therapy. You can start by contacting your health insurer to find names of therapists covered by your insurance plan. If you're covered by an integrated health care system such as Kaiser Permanente you can simply call the psychiatry department for an appointment. The Internet or Yellow Pages are also good places to look for cognitive-behavioral therapists. The Obsessive Compulsive Foundation's website (www.ocfoundation.org) can help locate therapists, as well as provide a wealth of other information. It also lists current research studies, which if you are able to participate in them, may include free treatment.

Self-Help

This workbook, of course, is a self-help manual primarily for people with mild to moderate symptoms. The treatment planning steps and methods here can help you significantly reduce the severity of your symptoms. Whatever your level of OCD, mild to extremely severe, this book will provide you with an understanding of the steps needed to feel better. This is accomplished in three ways. First, by understanding more about OCD, how common it is, and how it distorts thinking (especially risk/danger interpretation); you should feel less isolated and have a greater sense of control over your symptoms. Second, you'll learn three forms of treatment that work together to reduce your symptoms. Third, we'll help you create your own individualized treatment program to counteract OCD.

The three treatment methods you'll learn in this book are:

1. Cognitive therapy techniques
2. Exposure with response prevention (ERP)
3. The ORDER-ABC method

These methods play complementary roles in an integrated treatment program. We'll start by teaching you cognitive techniques. You'll identify thinking errors that amplify your discomfort and learn to correct them to reduce discomfort. This will help prepare you for ERP, a method of systematically confronting intrusive thoughts and images and getting control of compulsive behavior. The ORDER-ABC method teaches you to handle anxiety-provoking situations outside of your scheduled self-treatment sessions, or as you prepare to engage in ERP.

If you're inclined to give up or doubt your ability to do a self-help program on your own, hang in there and read this and the following chapter. In order to make a truly informed decision as to what treatment option is right for you, it's important that you know more about what the treatment entails and exactly what you need to do to put it into practice.

When it comes to the therapy for OCD described in this book, there's good news and bad news. The good news is actually excellent news. Of those who are able to commit themselves to therapy and see it through, 75 to 85 percent experience dramatic improvement. If you engage in the therapy we outline, you have an excellent chance of substantially reducing the discomfort you experience and the amount of time spent obsessing and ritualizing, which will significantly improve your quality of life.

The bad news is that in order to rewire your brain you need to activate the faulty circuits. That means therapy requires you to trigger the OCD, which will make you feel anxious or distressed. The idea of intentionally triggering OCD scares off about 25 percent of people who consider treatment. The result of that decision, however, is that they continue to feel anxious and suffer from OCD indefinitely. So the decision you face now is whether to be part of the group who are guaranteed to continue to suffer, or to be part of the group who get dramatically better.

Before we get to the specifics of treatment, however, there are some additional considerations that will help you be as well prepared as possible to engage in treatment. At the end of the self-assessment for treatment readiness, we'll have some specific recommendations depending on your readiness profile.

Obstacles to Treatment

Severe OCD Symptoms

If your OCD is severe, your first line of treatment should be to talk with a psychologist or psychiatrist well versed in OCD treatment. Severe symptoms render daily functioning extremely difficult. It's advisable to attend the appointment with a support person, if possible, to help you remember and accurately report the level and intensity of your symptoms. People with severe symptoms should use this book as a supplement to therapy, but it shouldn't be your main form of treatment.

Alcohol or Drug Problems

People sometimes turn to drugs and alcohol to try to manage their OCD. This frequently leads to substance abuse and dependency. OCD sufferers who struggle with alcohol or drug abuse should seek professional help to overcome those habits while simultaneously getting help for their OCD. If this is your situation, it is highly likely that as part of treatment you would be offered an SRI only after abstinence. You may find that medication reduces the discomfort of OCD, which in turn helps lower the likelihood of relapse. Having both of these problems at the same time is likely to lead to depression. Fortunately, SRIs can help with that also.

Depression

It is common for OCD sufferers to experience some degree of depression. Estimates vary, but approximately one-third of people with OCD struggle with severe depression, and up to 90 percent may have some level of depression. As you might imagine, it would be difficult, if not impossible, to engage in ERP while severely depressed. ERP requires energy, perseverance, and force of will, characteristics typically lacking in depression.

The following questions can help you determine whether you are depressed. If so, getting professional help is imperative to being able to proceed with OCD treatment.

Depression Symptom Self-Assessment

During the past two weeks, which of the following symptoms have you experienced more than half the days?

- **Feeling down, depressed, or hopeless most of the day**
- **Lack of interest or pleasure most of the day**
- **Feeling guilty or like a failure**
- **Sleeping too little or too much**
- **Feeling tired and fatigued**
- **Eating too little or too much, or unexplained weight loss or gain**
- **Poor concentration**
- **Being fidgety or restless, or the opposite, being slow or sluggish**
- **Thoughts of death or hurting or killing yourself**

Generally, a diagnosis of "major depression" would be indicated if you answered "yes" to a total of five questions, including one or both of the first two questions. "Major depression" is a fairly serious degree of depression, though depression of even lesser severity can be debilitating.

Although OCD can also generate some of these symptoms, the first three and the last one on the list are highly indicative of depression. (A notable exception is that some OCD sufferers are also plagued by thoughts that they might harm or kill themselves. The big difference between OCD and depression is that depressed people find the idea of death appealing, while people with OCD are *afraid* they might find it appealing.) If you are thinking of suicide, we strongly advise you to seek professional help NOW. Do not see how it goes. If there's any question as to whether you are generally depressed, a visit to a psychiatrist, primary care doctor, or psychotherapist would be a good place to start.

Depression is easier to treat than most people imagine, and it is enormously common. There are behavioral treatments for depression as well as treatment with the same SRI medications that can help control OCD symptoms.

Other Forms of Anxiety

Many OCD sufferers have an additional anxiety disorder. Brief definitions of the main forms of anxiety (other than OCD) are as follows:

- **Panic.** Intense, rapid onset of increased heart rate, shortness of breath, dizziness, and fear of passing out or dying, losing control, or going crazy. Symptoms are usually severe for ten to twenty minutes and then decrease back to baseline over the next half hour. People are often fatigued when the intense symptoms subside.

- **Social anxiety.** Fear and avoidance of being in groups of people due to feeling as though they are thinking about you and judging you negatively.

- **Agoraphobia.** Fear of being out in public due to concerns that something bad or catastrophic might happen to you. Often the danger is ill defined. People with this problem tend to travel only to familiar destinations, such as the homes of relatives, to work, and certain stores. New, unfamiliar destinations are avoided.

- **Specific phobia.** Fear of a particular situation, animal, or activity. Common phobias include spiders, rats, snakes, heights, air travel, small spaces, and needles.

- **PTSD.** Post-traumatic stress disorder can occur after a life-threatening event or one perceived as life threatening. Intrusive, fearful images occur during the day when triggered by a reminder of the event. Nightmares of the event are also common. PTSD is common after car accidents, robbery, assault, rape, domestic violence, living in a high-crime area or war zone, or experiencing combat.

The presence of another form of anxiety complicates the treatment of OCD, and guidelines for dealing with these other disorders are beyond the scope of this book. Professional assessment and treatment is highly recommended. If you suffer from phobias or any of the preceding forms of anxiety, we refer you to the *The Heal Your Anxiety Workbook* and other resources for help. If you are suffering from PTSD, turn to *Conquering Post-Traumatic Stress Disorder* and other resources for help.

Indecision

A notable obstacle to treatment among people with "the doubting disease" (as OCD is sometimes called) is indecisiveness. Difficultly making decisions is a symptom of OCD and needs to be recognized as such. If you are reading this and going back and forth between thinking self-help treatment is a good idea and then thinking it's not for you, that's exactly what one might expect of OCD. People with OCD often spend massive amounts of time gathering data in an effort to make the "correct" or "best" decision. Although good decisions require information, OCD can lead people to miss many a good opportunity for fear that it may not be "perfect." Life requires a certain degree of risk taking—there are no guarantees, nothing is certain. We cannot guarantee that this self-help program will work for you. We can, however, predict with high probability that without treatment your symptoms will either stay the same or get worse.

We encourage you to include a trusted friend or family member in your treatment planning and implementation. A good support person can play an invaluable role in helping you sort through your treatment options and cheer you on through the process.

Fatigue

OCD can be extremely taxing and lead to fatigue. The more severe the symptoms, the more likely fatigue is to result. If you are spending a couple of hours per day (or more) thinking about things that make you uncomfortable, anxious, or fearful, and a similar amount of time engaged in neutralizing rituals, it's no wonder you feel exhausted. Spending that much time on anything is like a part-time job, and the fact that the time is spent feeling bad simply compounds the toll it takes on your physical and mental energy reserves. Fatigue, of course, makes treatment more difficult. Recognizing OCD symptoms as a source of fatigue helps refute the common excuse for not beginning treatment, "I don't have the energy to do it," because the treatment is the answer to the problem. Treatment leads to greater energy as symptoms diminish, mental freedom increases, and time devoted to compulsions decreases.

Readiness for Treatment

Motivation for Change

A critical ingredient of any plan for successfully reducing or overcoming OCD is *your* motivation and commitment to change. It's normal for commitment to vary somewhat, especially when you're feeling anxious. Everyone has times of feeling more optimistic and stronger than other times. But even if your OCD is severe, you can dramatically reduce it and improve the quality of your life. So because you've started this book, we encourage you not only to continue, but also to dedicate yourself to improving your life over the next several weeks. You *can* do it. This workbook can help you. However, you're the only one who can do the actual work that leads to changing how your brain functions and to conquering OCD. So before we go any further, let's assess your readiness for change.

 READINESS FOR CHANGE WORKSHEET

Answer the following questions to get a sense of your readiness to begin reprogramming your brain.

(Circle one number for all questions with 1 through 5 answering options; 1 = no, 5 = definitely yes.)

Motivation

OCD gets in the way of things I want to do.

1—2—3—4—5

OCD gets in the way of how I want to feel.

1—2—3—4—5

OCD gets in the way of how I want to think.

1—2—3—4—5

I want more enjoyment from life.

1—2—3—4—5

Controlling OCD would give me a great sense of accomplishment.

1—2—3—4—5

I look forward to getting more done when I'm better able to direct my thoughts.

1—2—3—4—5

My family and loved ones will benefit when I have greater control.

1—2—3—4—5

Total _____ **÷ 7 = Average**

Willingness

I'm fed up with OCD and want to get better.

1—2—3—4—5

It means a lot to me to tackle this problem and make progress.

1—2—3—4—5

I've been strong enough to get through some bad episodes of OCD. I can certainly get through a treatment program.

1—2—3—4—5

I believe treatment can improve my life.

1—2—3—4—5

Even if I'm anxious about doing some of the exercises, I'm willing to do them.

1—2—3—4—5

Total _____ ÷ 5 = Average

Experience

I remember a time when I tackled a tough problem and made things better.

1—2—3—4—5

I sometimes think I can't do something, then find I can.

1—2—3—4—5

I've been in therapy for OCD before and know how to improve it.

1—2—3—4—5

I've read about OCD.

1—2—3—4—5

Total _____ ÷ 4 = Average

Support

People in my life are supportive of me getting better.

1—2—3—4—5

I have a close friend/family member who can help me.

1—2—3—4—5

I have a psychotherapist who can help me.

1—2—3—4—5

I've talked with my doctor or psychiatrist about OCD.

1—2—3—4—5

I'm taking medicine to control OCD.

1—2—3—4—5

I have (or plan to find) a support group.

1—2—3—4—5

Total _____ ÷ 6 = Average

Summary Chart

On the following chart, plot your average score for the answers you gave to the questions on the previous two pages: Motivation, Willingness, Experience, and Support. This will give you a quick understanding of your strengths and vulnerabilities before you proceed with self-treatment. Here is one person's summary chart. Fill in your own scores on the blank summary chart that follows.

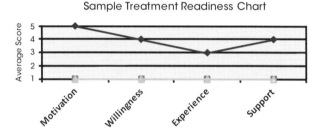

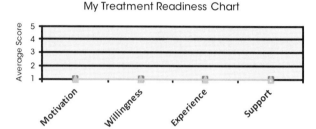

If your average score was three or higher in all categories, you are well prepared to continue on to treatment planning. If one or more average scores were less than three, some additional consideration should be given as to how to increase that particular level or compensate in some way. Here are some suggestions about how to interpret your scores and the actions to take.

Most people reading this workbook are likely to have average to above average motivation for treatment. If your average Motivation score is low, it might be that your OCD is not sufficiently severe or impactful to warrant treatment at this time. Look back at your responses on the Assessing the Impact Worksheet (page 19). If your answers indicate that you spend an hour or more each day on obsessions and compulsions, getting this under better control would have very definite benefits for your life. If OCD is having an impact yet your motivation is low, the most likely explanation is that you may be depressed. If this is the case for you, treatment for depression is indicated before going further with OCD treatment.

Willingness may wax and wane depending on how you feel on a given day. A low average score on Willingness might suggest that you fear the process of change or doubt that it could work for you. As we said earlier, OCD is called the "doubting disease." It's understandable (and somewhat predictable) that you might experience doubt prior to engaging in treatment. If your score was low, we suggest you spend time imagining what your life could be like without OCD. Talking with your support person(s) can also help you imagine a better future for yourself when OCD is under control. Chapter 5 contains information on cognitive therapy and on particular a topic called "thought distortions." That will probably be an important topic for you. It will help you look more closely at your beliefs about your obsessive thoughts and how those mistaken beliefs interfere with your willingness to change.

If your average score on Experience is low, that may be a function of how long and persistent anxiety and/or OCD have been a factor in your life. Very often people with a significant amount of anxiety are reluctant to take the kinds of risks that would build a history of succeeding at new challenges. It's important to know that the self-treatment program described in this workbook is done in a gradual manner. We'll help you build a treatment plan that will start off with challenges that you'll be willing to take and build up from there. That will help you gain confidence in your ability to successfully make positive changes. If your motivation is strong and your support network is good, this gradual method of working will probably be fine for you. If, in addition to low experience, motivation

and support are not strong, working with a professional psychotherapist would be highly desirable (see page 24 for how to choose a therapist).

As you can tell from the frequent references to support, it probably goes without saying that good support can make a huge difference in your ability to succeed in self-treatment. If your average Support score was low, give additional thought to who could be in your support network. Think about friends, family members, past teachers, or clergy, even if they don't live nearby but have encouraged you to take action in the past. They are likely still supportive even if by phone, email, or Internet chat. Many people are happy to help others—you might be surprised at the response you get if you ask. The best support person is one who is patient, warm, and willing to encourage you to go beyond your comfort level. Other resources to consider are local or online OCD support groups. And as we've stated before, if you don't have good support, the help of a professional trained in OCD therapy will undoubtedly make a big difference.

Now that you have a better idea of the treatment options, and have assessed your readiness to change, it's time to move on to learning how OCD develops and how you can rewire your brain so that you can be done with it.

Chapter 4
The ABCs of Allowing Your Brain to Change

You may ask yourself, "Why is my brain plagued by OCD while other people don't have to deal with this?" Or you may have wondered, "If OCD is a problem with my brain, will I suffer from this my entire life, no matter what kind of help I receive?" The answers to both questions will surprise you and give you hope.

Recent research in neuroscience has shed light on which parts of the brain are most active in people suffering from OCD. There is also good news about what you can do to strengthen those parts of your brain that have not been functioning up to par, so that OCD becomes less and less of a problem. And you will learn how to do just that in this workbook. By learning how your brain changes and by doing the exercises in these pages, you can **A**llow your **B**rain to **C**hange so that OCD fades out of your life. The letters ABC, as we use them here, will help you remember the importance of allowing your brain to change as you adjust to new ways of thinking and behaving.

In this chapter, you'll come to understand the ABCs of rewiring your brain by learning the following:

- **Some basics about how your brain works**
- **The parts of your brain that contribute to OCD**
- **How your brain can be rewired**
- **The things you need to do to rewire OCD out of your life**

Don't worry, we aren't going to bombard you with a lot of technical information that will be hard to understand or be irrelevant to OCD. You'll learn some important facts about your brain that will put OCD into perspective and make the exercises that follow understandable. Many people who attend our classes say that when they hear about how their brain works it demystifies the exercises we are asking them to perform. Think of this chapter as a brief owner's manual on how to operate your brain more efficiently so that you won't suffer from OCD.

Introducing Your Brain

Although your brain weighs only three pounds, it has 100 billion nerve cells called *neurons*, and many more support cells. Each of your 100 billion neurons is capable of maintaining connections with about 10,000 other neurons. The quality and type of connection they make can create or do away with OCD. Your neurons make those connections with one another by sending chemicals called *neurotransmitters* across a gap called a *synapse*.

The neurotransmitters called GABA (gamma-aminobutryic acid) and serotonin are the ones that you want to work more efficiently in your brain because they promote calmness, a better mood, and less OCD.

Your right hemisphere is where information is synthesized into the "whole picture," which allows you to get the gist of a situation. It is generally more creative and activates when you are learning something new. Once you learn a skill, it is encoded into your left hemisphere, where routines, linear sequencing, and language are processed. Generally, your right hemisphere processes negative emotions while your left hemisphere processes positive emotions.

Within your brain are four structures that play major roles in OCD. They are the *striatum, amygdala, hippocampus,* and *orbital frontal cortex.* Your orbital frontal cortex (right behind the orbs of your eyes) helps control emotions, if trained properly. During OCD, your orbital frontal cortex gets flooded with information, as though a gate had been left open.

This results in a discrepancy between what you know is the right, or normal, thing to do, and what you are feeling compelled to do—engage in compulsive behaviors to "make things right."

Your orbital frontal cortex can also be hijacked by your amygdala. Your amygdala is the center of fear and tends to be hypersensitive in people with anxiety disorders such as OCD. Your amygdala is involved in your emotional memory and reacts unconsciously to events and situations that you feel are potentially dangerous. It is a principal player in the *fear circuit* in your brain, and triggers the fight-or-flight response through your *hypothalamic pituitary adrenal axis (HPA).*

Here's how it works: First the amygdala signals your hypothalamus (another part of your brain) to secrete a substance called cortical-releasing factor, or CRF, which in turn triggers your pituitary gland to release another substance called ACTH (adrenocorticotropic hormone) into your bloodstream. This triggers your adrenal glands to release two other hormones, epinephrine (adrenaline) and norepinephrine, which charges up your sympathetic nervous system (which we will describe below). About thirty minutes later, a stress hormone called cortisol is released. All of this further excites your amygdala to keep the fear circuit going.

Unfortunately, you've never learned to turn off the fear circuit naturally by exposing yourself to your fears. Instead, you've used "escape" and "avoidance" habits— your compulsive behaviors—over and over again. Ironically (as we will describe later), these behaviors actually contribute to a more easily triggered fear network.

Fortunately, your orbital frontal cortex can learn to inhibit the overactivity of your amygdala and the fear network.

The connections between your orbital frontal lobe and amygdala strengthen as you learn how to become relaxed instead of anxious and how to stop engaging in compulsive behaviors. Other parts of your brain help your orbital frontal lobe regain its mastery over the fear network. Your hippocampus (the part of the brain most involved in creating and storing memories) provides context and helps you remember what is worthy of fear and what is not.

Other parts of your nervous system must be brought into balance, too. Your autonomic nervous system has two branches: the *sympathetic* nervous system, which regulates arousal, and the *parasympathetic* nervous system, which regulates relaxation.

Your sympathetic branch activates your brain and body with the neurotransmitters norepinephrine and epinephrine (adrenaline). The parasympathetic branch helps you calm down by releasing the brain neurotransmitter GABA, which acts to dampen the effects of adrenaline and also calm down your amygdala. In this workbook, you'll learn how to turn on your parasympathetic system.

One of the reasons that OCD is so uncomfortable is that when our fear circuit gets hyperactive it overactivates our sympathetic nervous system. The results of this activation are:

- Heart rate increases
- Blood vessels narrow
- Blood pressure increases
- Breathing gets shallow
- Muscles tighten
- Adrenal gland releases adrenaline and cortisol into the bloodstream

When you're in an activated OCD brain loop worrying about something (e.g., potential germs on the kitchen counter), your brain activates this fear circuit. As the fearful scenario ratchets up in your mind, the fight-or-flight response also ratchets up. Your brain–

body systems are pretty complex. But your frontal lobes (your thinking brain) exert a weak force on the primitive amygdala and striatum. You need to exercise that connection to get it stronger and more automatic, so that when you want to control OCD, that connection functions better than it does now.

Your hippocampus can help deactivate your amygdala. Because scary thoughts activate the amygdala, more realistic and calming thoughts can help deactivate it. You can remind yourself that OCD thoughts and impulses are adrenaline-induced false alarms and that "nothing bad happened the last time I ignored them." By ignoring your false alarms again and again and living through the OCD storm, you will increasingly strengthen the downward control connections between your orbital frontal cortex and your amygdala and your conscious brain's brake mechanism. Although this may sound a bit scientific and theoretical, in coming chapters we'll get much more specific as to how you can put this into practice to achieve your goal of reducing your OCD and feeling better.

Teaching Your Brain to Neutralize Doubt

OCD has been called the "doubting disease" because you may constantly doubt yourself. You doubt your self-control, intentions, morality, memory, and on and on. If you're a washer, you doubt your body's ability to block infection and doubt that you washed your hands adequately. If you're a checker, you doubt that you turned off the stove. Or you may doubt that you are a moral, loving person when you have what for others would be a fleeting violent thought or an unsanctioned sexual desire. Or you may doubt that you are a law-abiding person and doubt that you can be trusted to hold your baby, or to drive your car safely, without swerving into onrushing traffic.

Doubt, for you, may lead to extraordinary lengths to calm and reassure yourself. Why does a disturbing thought turn into a firestorm? Your amygdala gets sensory information before any of the higher, more developed parts of the brain, such as your orbital frontal cortex. It even monitors your thoughts. If your amygdala recognizes something even slightly associated with danger, it sets off a powerful chain reaction (your fear network) that focuses the mind and body to deal with the perceived threat. In OCD it appears that the "on switch" of this threat threshold has been set way, way too low. That is, all kinds of nonthreatening things trigger your amygdala to turn on its response.

In addition to needing to rewire the amygdala's on switch, you'll need to rewire its off switch. In contrast to the on switch, the off switch is set way, way too high. So once your brain's frontal lobes analyze the information or thought that triggered the amygdala, and determine that there really isn't a threat, this part of your brain has tremendous difficulty doing its job of turning off the amygdala's response.

Imagine if your home heating system were controlled by a thermostat that is supposed to keep your home between 68°F and 70°F (20°C and 21°C). However, when the temperature drops below 68°F (20°C), it turns the furnace on and won't stop until your house reaches 100°F (38°C). You might say, "Well, that'll keep us from getting cold!" and you'd certainly be right about that. But it wouldn't keep you from being extremely uncomfortable most of the time and wasting a lot of energy, too.

More than likely, after living in such a home, you'd start to feel a bit chilly when the temperature got down around 80°F (27°C). (Or as this applies to OCD, you might feel dirty after simply touching something that was on the floor.)

Another part of your brain that needs to be rewired is the striatum. This is the part responsible for letting the gate open that allows nuisance obsessions to flood your orbital frontal cortex and quickly trigger "automatic" compulsive behaviors. If the striatum is working well, there is no OCD. Normally, you don't need to give much thought to these automatic behaviors. They are well practiced and ready for use. They enable us to do things such as ride a bike or drive a car while thinking about something totally unrelated. Once the automatic program is running, your conscious mind is free to do something else.

For instance, when normal hand washing behavior gets triggered, you follow a set routine: turn on the water, wet your hands, soap them, scrub for several seconds, rinse your hands, turn off the water, and then dry your hands. While you're washing your hands you don't need to be totally focused on it; you could be thinking about a friend you're about to go see. This hand washing program then terminates and allows the next behavior to begin. Often with OCD, however, this program doesn't terminate and the whole thing needs to start again and perhaps be done ten times or for ten minutes or some other "magical" termination point. And the whole time your conscious mind is preoccupied with the act of washing.

This gets very confusing because in OCD this part of your brain works just fine for most things, but when it comes to particular topics, especially those that trigger your amygdala, your striatum gets stuck open. Try as you may, your amygdala doesn't terminate this OCD loop until it feels satisfied that the danger has passed.

By combining the actions of the amygdala and the striatum, we get something like the following scenario. You're making lunch and get some mustard on your fingers. You notice that this feels a bit yucky and have the thought, "I don't like how that feels." Your amygdala, which has its threshold set way, way too low, then triggers a small response that focuses your mind on the question: "Is this dangerous?"

Your amygdala now becomes the master of your brain. All resources are dedicated to solving this potential security breach. Your conscious mind starts to review everything you've heard lately about food safety. Has mustard been in the news? Have there been any product recalls? What if this mustard is old and grew some harmful bacteria? Aha, harmful bacteria! Your amygdala is monitoring your thoughts and detects this more serious level of potential threat. It escalates its response and "turns up the heat." The automatic hand washing program gets triggered to take care of the problem, and off you go to the sink. Your amygdala, however, hasn't reached "100°F" yet, so it still has control of your brain's resources. Your conscious mind is working on this problem of food safety. If the mustard is loaded with bacteria, could it penetrate my skin? (90°F.) What if I don't get it all off of me and touch my daughter? (95°F.) She might die! (99°F.) And it would be my fault. (100°F!) The amygdala continues to stimulate the striatum's problem-solving program—hand washing—until it eventually exhausts its response. Then you finally get the feeling that your hands are clean, and you can stop washing and go on to the next thing.

The important thing to note is that when you get stuck in one of these loops you need to use your orbital frontal cortex and hippocampus functions to break out. It's like you need to consciously take hold of the manual control switch and pull hard. Part of the problem, however, is that your amygdala is so powerful and unused to having its signal challenged that you immediately begin to doubt whether you should pull the manual switch or obey your amygdala's danger signal. When everything is working as it should, listening to the amygdala is a good thing. When you know that you're dealing with OCD, however, then you know the kinds of circumstances, thoughts, and feelings that are part of this *erroneous* danger signal. That is, it isn't a danger signal at all. It's a false alarm that causes havoc in your life.

How Your Brain Changes

The ABC of getting OCD rewired out of your life takes place in the areas of the brain on the level of the synapses. The rewiring of your synapses is possible through a process called *neuroplasticity*. Neuroplasticity means that your neurons can form new connections with one another while older, less useful connections fade away from lack of use. As you learned earlier in the chapter, your synapses are the gaps between your neurons. Neuroplasticity occurs on the synaptic level (which is why neuroplasticity is some-times called synaptic plasticity).

The phrase *Cells that fire together, wire together* describes how your brain (through your synapses) reorganizes itself through neuroplasticity as you learn new things. Neuroplasticity is what makes memory and all new learning possible, including breaking old habits (including OCD).

This is how your brain changes. You can remember this by the acronym ABC, or:

A—Allow your

B—Brain to

C—Change

ABC, too, is accomplished through neuroplasticity. Your brain changes its synapses when you remember something new. Your brain would not learn anything new if it were entirely and permanently hardwired. Learning something new is the process of rewiring your brain.

By practicing the techniques that you will learn in this workbook, you will train your neurons to fire together and wire together to be calmer and not obsess and engage in compulsive behaviors. The more frequently neurons fire together, the greater the chance that they will fire together in the future and produce calmness instead of obsessing and performing compulsive behaviors.

The more you practice a new behavior, the more likely you'll do it in the future. That's why baseball players go to batting practice and musicians spend so much time playing their instruments. Neuroplasticity occurs when you do something over and over again. In other words, repetition rewires your brain and creates habits. Think of it this way—water flows downhill, not uphill. Your brain does what it is used to doing.

Right now it is used to having obsessive thoughts and performing compulsive behaviors. If you want to change what it is used to doing, you'll need to make a strong effort to do what you don't feel like doing, then repeat that new behavior often. Eventually, you'll repeat it without much effort. This means that the more you practice feeling relaxed instead of feeling anxious and resist the drive to engage in compulsive behaviors, the sooner you'll extinguish your OCD. All this is possible because you can decide to override the overactivity of your amygdala, and teach your striatum to filter out nuisance thoughts and compulsive behaviors by activating your orbital frontal lobes and hippocampus to exert their full powers. The more you practice the techniques you'll learn in this workbook, the less plagued by OCD you'll be.

You know from past experience that your obsessive thoughts and compulsive behaviors do not make sense. You need to thoroughly weave this fact into your memory so that when OCD strikes, you'll be able to exert frontal lobe (conscious, intentional) control to pull the plug on the obsessions and compulsive behaviors.

The information and exercises in the following chapters will familiarize you with how OCD works and, most important, how *your* OCD works. There will be times during your self-treatment program when you will need to draw on this knowledge to give you additional strength and courage. Your rational mind is what will enable you to turn down the thermostat on your amygdala and overcome this disorder.

Although there was a fair amount of information on the ABC technique above, there are a few critical points that will be important for you to remember. They are:

- **Your brain is a complex organ that *can* change through neuroplasticity if you practice the exercises in this workbook.**
- **If you keep doing what comes easily for you, your OCD will continue.**
- **To conquer OCD, you'll have to do some new things, and they won't all be easy.**
- **By practicing the new behaviors you will learn in this book you create the conditions that Allow your Brain to Change.**
- **Because ABC isn't an instant process, you'll need to repeat the skills you learn in this workbook over and over again. This will lead to solid and enduring rewiring of new, more comfortable and more satisfying habits.**

Chapter 5

The ABCs of Changing Your Thinking

Allow Your Brain to Change Thinking Errors

We all engage in what are called "thinking errors," or "thought distortions." These are patterns of thinking that everyone falls into when we're nervous, stressed, sad, or depressed. These thoughts are generally very believable, quite persuasive, and harshly negative, and they make our lives more difficult than they need to be. We know you are a victim of these kinds of thoughts because we *all* are. The fact is, however, obsessive thinking makes you more susceptible than others to this particular thought pattern. Even if you don't fully believe your obsessive thoughts (which is good), the sheer repetitive nature of them usually means they'll get the upper hand most of the time. Then you engage in your compulsive behavior to get the obsessive thoughts to stop.

This chapter is about the ABCs of "cognitive therapy." Cognitive therapy is a way to change the way your brain works. This in turn will change the thoughts you have and lessen the frequency and intensity of your obsessions. We do this by tackling your thinking errors. First, you need to know what thinking errors are, which type you use, and how they make your OCD worse. As you master the information in this chapter, you will be in a much better position to get your OCD under control. By following the examples in this chapter and practicing the new thought patterns you define for yourself, you'll set the conditions that will Allow your Brain to Change. In the next section, we'll present an example of what thinking errors are like and how we can work with them.

Working on Your Thinking Errors

Ever since she was a young child, Kathryn liked things to be "just right." As a teenager she began calling herself "a perfectionist," in part to blunt criticism from other children about her need for her schoolwork to be double- and triple-checked, her clothing clean and unwrinkled, her locker exceedingly neat, her gym clothes always spotlessly clean, and so on.

As an adult, she was often distracted when talking with colleagues in their offices at the insurance company where she worked. There were times when she was so focused on stacks of unfiled papers and other clutter there that she couldn't concentrate. One day one of her colleagues said, "Earth to Kathryn. Are you there?"

She couldn't help herself and blurted out, "I don't know how you can work in this mess."

"What are you talking about?" he asked.

Kathryn didn't mean it as an insult, but she had decided long ago that she couldn't work unless everything in the office or room was in its place. To her, things that were "left lying around" seemed to be crying out for attention.

The next meeting took place in her immaculate office. She had spent hours and hours rewriting one page of the company policy and procedures manual. She found herself bogged down on one particular paragraph and had trouble moving on to the rest of the document. She'd been obsessing on it for days. In fact, during dinner the previous night her husband asked that she stop talking about it. As they sat down for the meeting, one of her colleagues placed his papers on her desk. She glanced at the papers, then him, then the papers again. "Are you just going to leave them there?" she asked, with visible irritation.

He shook his head, then picked them up and placed them in his lap. To punctuate his displeasure he glanced at his colleagues, subtly shaking his head. She began the meeting by pointing out the paragraph that upset her and said, "This has got to change or the whole document will have to be thrown out."

"Are you joking?" her colleague asked. "What is going on with you? First you couldn't meet in Brenda's office because it wasn't antiseptic like yours and now you're hung up on a paragraph about the parking lot." He nodded to his colleagues, stood up, and the others followed him out of the office.

Later that day Kathryn's regional manager called her into his office. Kathryn started defensively, "If this is about my coworkers, I want to stop you right there. They just don't have the attention to detail I do. I'm a perfectionist and they just can't handle that. You need to talk to *them*."

He looked disappointed by her comment. "I have. That's the problem."

Kathryn went home that night wondering how much longer she could hold her job. She knew that she had spent far too long on the paragraph about the parking lot. Yet at the same time she told herself that if the procedure was not worded exactly right, people would not follow it, and she would have done a poor-quality job, when she owed it to her employer to do a perfect one. She also knew from her own experience that she had to get it "just right" or she simply would not be able to move on. She was terrified that if her manager ever knew the degree to which her perfectionism slowed her work, she would be fired. As a defense, she tried hard to portray her perfectionism as an asset to the company.

Perfectionism is a form of OCD as well as a type of thinking error. To the degree that you believe your thinking errors, they have power over you and make OCD more difficult to treat. To the degree you recognize that some of your thoughts are thinking errors, you have power to stop them. If you simply accept them and believe them, your OCD will be much more difficult to control. This chapter will help you identify your thinking errors and revise them so that your thoughts can be a help rather than a hindrance. As you read the definitions and examples of thinking errors below, you'll find that Kathryn's thinking contained several. Common types of thinking errors that perpetuate OCD include:

1. **Either/or thinking.** You think things are right or wrong, clean or contaminated, safe or dangerous, black or white. This type of thinking error doesn't leave room for gray. Because nothing in this world is completely right, clean, or safe, people with this type of thinking error generally feel anxious a good deal of the time. This leads to the desire to ritualize in order to temporarily reduce the tension. Examples: "If the mirror hangs perfectly straight, I'll feel good. If it's crooked, I'll feel bad until I can fix it." "If I don't put my clothes on in the right sequence, I can't leave the house." For Kathryn, things were either perfect or completely unacceptable.

2. **Overestimating the probability of risk.** You imagine that if something *could* go wrong, it *will* go wrong. You interpret low-probability events as high-probability events. Examples: "If I forget to lock the second-floor windows, a burglar will get in." "I need to check my daughter's food very carefully to make sure there's no broken glass in it." "My boss wants to see me—I'm probably going to get fired."

3. **Catastrophizing/overestimating the severity of risk.** This involves turning situations into worst-case scenarios. Examples: "That woman in the elevator coughed. She probably has tuberculosis.

And now I've got it." "I used a public toilet. People with AIDS probably sat on it. I've got to get to the doctor and get tested." "I think I left the toaster plugged in. My family will be in danger unless I go home and unplug it!" This type of thinking error often goes hand in hand with **overestimating the probability of risk.**

4. **Emotional reasoning.** You regard an emotion as evidence of the truth, instead of looking at the facts. How you feel internally gets mistaken for external reality. Examples: "I have this sick feeling in my stomach—I've got to go to my daughter's school. I know she's in terrible danger." "I feel scared suddenly. Something must have happened to my husband on his business trip." When Kathryn felt uncomfortable, she was certain that everything had to stop until that one thing was fixed. The problem is that these gut feelings are usually false alarms that get triggered for no particular reason.

5. **Overgeneralizing.** Words that serve as a tip-off that this error is occurring are: always, never, forever, all, none, completely, totally, no one, everyone. Examples: "You always do that." "I'll never be able to get OCD under control." "I'm a complete failure." "My life is ruined, forever." Kathryn was guilty of overgeneralizing when she felt the entire procedure manual had to be thrown out due to a problem with one section.

6. **Magical thinking.** Magical thinking is similar to "superstition." You make connections between

things or events when there is no logical reason to do so, or the connections only make sense through a string of implausible "what-if" statements. Magical thinking increases anxiety by making its causes intangible and not based on reality. Examples: "If I tap seven times my child will be protected on the way home from school." "If I say this prayer three times, I'll get to work without having a car accident." This is a common thinking error for people with contamination obsessions. Examples: "What if one of the homeless people near the post office has tuberculosis and coughs and those germs get in the building and on the letters. When the mail carrier brings my mail, if I breathe the air near the letter I might get TB, too." "If I hug my nephew after touching a gas pump, the germs will get on him and he'll get sick."

7. **Need for certainty/persistent doubting.** This is characterized by a lack of tolerance for uncertainty. We all want a greater sense of certainty in our lives, but people who are prone to this thought distortion get highly anxious when there is no way to know something. They ask questions of themselves and others to try to obtain reassurance. No matter how much reassurance is given, the doubt and questions continue. Examples: "The doctors said my heart is fine, but I think they're wrong. I need to get a fifth opinion." "I think I locked the door, but I'm not sure. I better check again." "Are you sure we didn't hit a pedestrian back there? I heard a bumping noise. I didn't see anyone, but we should go back." "Are you *sure* I'm not sick?"

8. **Excessive responsibility.** This is the feeling that you are responsible for everyone's safety and well-being. It includes the illusion that it's possible to control every consequence of your actions. Examples: "I allowed the children to play in the sandbox and my niece cut her knee. My sister will never trust me to watch her again. If her knee gets infected it will be my fault." "My son got detention at school. I'm a disaster as a father." You are not in total control of the events in your life, never have been, and never will be. You can have a certain amount of control over some aspects of events, but never complete control.

9. **Overvalued thoughts.** This is the belief that if you think something, it must be true and must mean something about you for having thought it. Examples: "I imagined myself killing my child. I must be crazy. No one but a psycho-killer would think a thing like that." That interpretation is completely wrong. This was demonstrated by a scientific study in which "normal" people and those with OCD wrote down their thoughts over a period of several hours. A panel of psychologists could not tell the difference between them. This means that "normal" people have thoughts like the above also. The difference between "normal" and OCD thoughts appears to be the importance that people assign to them. People with OCD believe that having such a thought means they are bad people. Other people just dismiss the thought as weird, then go about what they were doing.

10. **Thought-action fusion.** This is the belief that thinking about something means that it did happen, or will cause it to happen. Thinking is the same as doing. Examples: "I think I pushed a man from the train platform and he was killed by the train. I called the police to report myself." "I had an urge to shout obscenities in church, so I stopped going. I can't bear to face those people." "In a moment of anger, I wished my father would drop dead. I've been saying the rosary five times a day to keep it from happening."

11. **Perfectionism.** This is the belief that everything in your control must be "perfect" or "just so." Some people are worried that they'll get in trouble for making a mistake; others can't tolerate the discomfort of things not meeting their unreasonably high standards. Examples: "My bed has to be made as soon as I get up. The bedspread has to hang down equally on both sides, with no wrinkles or creases. If the kids even get near the bed after it is made, I go into a panic." "I can't email a memo unless I'm certain there are no typos." "I've got to park my car perfectly straight in the parking space with the bumper just over the curb." People have wrinkles in their bedspreads, send out memos with errors, and park askew all the time and nothing bad happens to them. Kathryn, however, was unable to sit comfortably in an office that was messy or proceed on a document that had minor flaws.

12. **Inability to tolerate anxiety or discomfort.** This is the belief that feeling uncomfortable is never okay and needs to be avoided or terminated rather than tolerated. In its extreme form, this might be a fear of going crazy or losing control if the anxiety goes on too long or seems inescapable. Examples: "I can't take this feeling another second. I've got to wash my hands or I'll go crazy." "We have to go home. I can't possibly enjoy the movie. You know how nervous I get in crowded rooms."

13. **Focusing on the negative.** This is the belief that no matter how many things went right, the only things worth paying attention to are the ones that went wrong. When we think repeatedly about negative events and situations, our dominant emotions are negative. Examples: "My job evaluation was good except for one item. I can't stop thinking about what a failure I am." "Everything was great until it started raining—now the day is ruined."

14. **Predicting the future.** This is the belief that you know what will happen in the future. People who do this generally predict negative outcomes that interfere with trying something new and learning new things. Examples: "There's no use in even trying. I know I can't do it." "There's no way my OCD is going to get better." "Even if I am healthy now, I know I'm going to die a painful death from cancer."

Go back over the list of thinking errors and put an asterisk next to the three that sound most familiar to you. It's likely that these are the ones you use most often. Then rank them one to three. Think of recent examples of how these thinking errors affected you. Read the following list to jog your memory of ways you might mislabel your experience.

Inventory Your Thoughts and Beliefs

I feel terrible if things aren't just right. . . . .True or False

I should always be perfect. . . . . .True or False

I must be in control of my thoughts. . . . . . .True or False

I must make sure everything is in
perfect order. . . . . .True or False

If I miss a step in my routine it'll cause
a bad day. . . . . .True or False

My thoughts can trigger harm/an
accident/other bad outcome. . . . . .True or False

I've got to keep my thoughts clean
and pure. . . . . .True or False

A horrible thought about someone
can harm him or her. . . . . .True or False

There is something fundamentally
wrong with me. . . . . .True or False

I've got to know ahead of time what's
going to happen. .True or False

I need to be 100 percent certain that
everything will be okay. . . . . .True or False

If someone with a cold walks into
the room I'll get sick. . . . . .True or False

If I have a cut on my finger, it may
get gangrene. . . . . .True or False

When I get ill, I wonder if I will die. . . . . . . .True or False

At restaurants, I could catch AIDS or
other diseases. . . . . .True or False

When someone says something harsh
or mean to me, I obsess about it. . . . . . . .True or False

I worry all the time that I will do
something bad. . . . . .True or False

People may suffer from my mistakes. . . . . .True or False

When I imagine something, I'm
convinced I'll do it. . . . . .True or False

If people knew my thoughts, they
would know I'm bad. . . . . .True or False

When I count or tap, I can ward off
bad things. . . . . .True or False

My morning ritual must be done or
it will be a bad day. . . . . .True or False

If something bad happens, it
happens to me. . . . . .True or False

I count on the worst to happen. . . . . .True or False

My luck is worse than most people's. . . . . .True or False

Things tend to go wrong, so I try to
keep them right. . . . . .True or False

If I'm anxious, I do my rituals. . . . . .True or False

The only way I can combat anxiety
is with my rituals. . . . . .True or False

If I have control, I have less anxiety. . . . . . .True or False

People we have treated for OCD tend to answer "true" to several of the previous statements. If you answered "true" to any of them, you are setting yourself up to feel more anxious and less in control of OCD. This is because you box yourself in with expectations that give you little flexibility. We'll help you restructure some of your beliefs to give yourself a fighting chance to better manage OCD. In the space below, list examples of your own thoughts and identify the type of thinking error they demonstrate. If you need a reminder of the types, reread the definitions. Pay special attention to the "top three" thinking errors that you asterisked.

MY THOUGHTS	TYPE OF THINKING ERROR

You are the narrator of your own life. Our minds offer up a constant stream of thoughts as we go through our day's activities. The tone and perspective you use to describe each experience generates feelings. For example, if you find yourself constantly telling yourself, "I can't function in a messy office," or "It looks like this is going to turn out badly," you'll generate anxious feelings. Underlying this narration are thought patterns that provide context to your experience and shape its meaning. Think of these thought patterns as having three main layers: automatic thoughts, assumptions, and core beliefs. Each of these layers goes deeper and makes your pattern of thinking more predictable, more familiar, more rigid. If you're happy most of the time, you probably don't want to change this underlying structure. If you're anxious, uncomfortable, or depressed much of the time, this structure can be improved. Let's look at those layers.

Working on Your Automatic Thoughts

On the surface are your *automatic thoughts.* These are like headlines that momentarily flash through your mind. Automatic thoughts are a form of "self-talk" that you use to interpret events of the day. You generate thousands of these every day. Automatic thoughts that fuel anxiety go something like this: You walk into a room, see things have been rearranged, and think, "Oh no, I don't like this. It's all wrong. I need to fix it" or "I need to arrange things the way they *should* be." These types of automatic thoughts are bad habits that cloud fresh and potentially positive experiences.

Your job is to replace bad thinking habits with good thinking habits, by generating new automatic thoughts to refute and contradict the old negative automatic thoughts. If you don't change your thinking—and the negative self-talk that goes with those thinking errors—your old automatic thoughts will continue to perpetuate your OCD.

In the left column that follows, you'll find examples of negative automatic thoughts. In the right column are alternatives you can use to refute those automatic thoughts. Which would you rather think? Which do you think can help you avoid obsessing, and return your thoughts to the task at hand?

CORRECTIVE THOUGHTS CHART

OLD AUTOMATIC THOUGHTS	NEW CORRECTIVE THOUGHTS
Here comes my obsessing again.	This happened before and I survived.
Something terrible will happen if I don't do my ritual.	I'm being superstitious. It's just an uncomfortable feeling in my body.
I'll catch AIDS by using a public toilet.	That's ridiculous. That's not how AIDS is transmitted. There's never been a single reported case of someone getting AIDS from a toilet.
I need to count all the red cars on the road.	That's a waste of my energy. Don't do it and the urge will pass.
I'm a hopeless mess.	I can and will help myself.
I've got to arrange all the papers on my desk before I leave.	Nothing in this world is perfect and that's okay.
I feel like something bad is going to happen.	No one can predict the future.
I probably have a brain tumor.	Brain tumors are very rare. It's far more likely that this is just a normal headache.
I'll always suffer from OCD. This book can't help me.	Thousands of people with OCD have gotten better. I can, too!

Do any of these negative thoughts sound familiar? Notice how the corrective thoughts give you flexibility and freedom from obsessions and compulsions. The corrective thoughts directly challenge the negative automatic thoughts. Use the following worksheet to give yourself some reality and hope. Transfer the thoughts that fuel your OCD from the Thinking Errors Chart to the chart below. Then refute them with new corrective thoughts. Make sure the corrective thoughts are true statements that promote flexibility and adaptability, and help you feel better.

Be sure to use "I" statements in the present tense when you write your new corrective thoughts. This helps make them more powerful when you say them to yourself, and they will give you a new set of more positive automatic thoughts.

When you trigger one of your old automatic thoughts, correct it with the positive one. Copy this list and carry it with you, so that you can refer to it. Review this list often, so that these more positive thoughts become your new automatic thoughts.

OLD AUTOMATIC THOUGHTS	NEW CORRECTIVE THOUGHTS

You can develop a variety of automatic thoughts that will serve you much better than those that trigger obsessions and compulsions. If you have trouble thinking of new thoughts to refute your old ones, read over the list below and see whether there are some ideas that can help you. Even if you think this won't work (which in itself is a negative automatic thought, an example of the thinking errors "focusing on the negative" and "predicting the future"), give it a try.

- I don't need to clean today. I've cleaned enough.
- I can cope with how things turn out if I don't count.
- Things are never perfect and that's just fine.
- I'll do the best that I can and that's enough.
- This will be a valuable learning experience.
- I can learn to live with shades of gray.
- I'll use my realistic mind to judge the situation, not my negative automatic OCD thoughts.
- I can learn to be more accepting of imperfections.
- My thoughts are just my thoughts.
- I can adapt to this situation, even if I don't like it.
- I've washed my hands once and that's enough.
- I'm not responsible for things I can do nothing about.
- Although I feel like something bad will happen, it's just a feeling. I can't predict the future.
- This is just my OCD acting up again.

Take a moment to write three new positive thoughts on an index card and carry it with you during the coming week. Read it on a regular basis, so that your brain can rewire and make them new habits. Practice self-talk using them, so that they become new *automatic* thoughts. Approach this exercise by developing automatic thoughts that are positive, hopeful, optimistic, and adaptive. Practice this and Allow your Brain to Change.

Working on Your Assumptions

Your *assumptions* are positioned between your automatic thoughts and core beliefs (which we'll discuss next). Assumptions aren't as fundamental as core beliefs, yet they aren't as obvious or familiar as automatic thoughts. They build on one another, with automatic thoughts resting on a foundation of assumptions.

Assumptions are like mini theories about your environment and yourself. Self-limiting assumptions are laced with words such as should, never, always, and must. For example, you might say to yourself "I *always* need to know exactly what will happen before I do anything." This assumption boxes you into feeling nervous about any situation because it's impossible to know what might happen. The assumptions "I *never* do well with change,"

or "I *always* need to be in control to feel comfortable" set any new situation beyond your comfort level.

Negative assumptions are rigid and inflexible and give you few options to succeed. As a result, you feel tense and anxious. You need to change your assumptions, so that they are flexible and reasonable. You need to modify your assumptions, so that they serve you well and are based on reality. They need to be adaptable, too, to give you the opportunity to cope with changing conditions.

Assumptions are the layer beneath automatic thoughts. Automatic thoughts are self-talk you use in *particular situations*; assumptions are theories that you carry with you in *many situations*. The following chart lists some examples of assumptions.

CORRECTIVE ASSUMPTIONS CHART

OLD NEGATIVE ASSUMPTIONS	NEW CORRECTIVE ASSUMPTIONS
I must always be certain.	There is no such thing as certainty.
I harm others with my thoughts and actions.	I am a peaceful, gentle person. I harm no one.
Bad thoughts are the same as bad actions.	Thoughts are only thoughts. They are fleeting and temporary.
It is intolerable/unforgivable to make a mistake.	Everyone makes mistakes. We can learn from mistakes.
I can't tolerate feeling anxious.	I can tolerate anxiety. I've lived through it many times before. I can do it again.
The world is a dangerous place.	The world is full of caring people and wonderful surprises.
Germs and dirt are very dangerous.	I have natural defenses against germs and dirt.
I must be perfect.	No one is perfect.
Things will go wrong if I don't do my rituals.	Rituals perpetuate my OCD.
I can cope only if things are clean/perfect/ordered/safe/secure, etc.	I can cope with uncertainty.
I'm extremely vulnerable to diseases.	I was healthy before all my rituals; I'll be fine without them.
I must make up for the imperfections in the world.	The world is an imperfect place. I'm not in charge.
God wants me to keep my thoughts pure.	My human impulses may lead to thoughts I don't intend to dwell on.
I am responsible for everyone's safety.	I can only do so much.
Thoughts like these mean I'm bad/crazy/evil.	Everyone has weird thoughts. I don't need to dwell on mine.
Nothing will ever turn out right for me.	I can't predict the future.
I'm a perfectionist.	Perfection doesn't exist.
I'm responsible for everything.	I'll do my part and allow others to do theirs.
Doubting is a good way to find flaws.	I will find the positive.
Doubting keeps me safe.	I know how to take care of myself.
I should be able to do things perfectly.	I will allow myself to be human.
My rituals prevent the worst from happening.	My rituals are a waste of time.
Bad things happen without my rituals.	Good and bad things happen despite my rituals.
There is always something wrong.	There's always something right.
My future needs to be protected.	I can write my own future.
OCD is who I am.	OCD is a bad habit that I'll break.
OCD is a family tradition.	It is a tradition that I will leave.
I'm a worrier.	I will learn to worry less.

You've probably got plenty of your own assumptions. Use the following worksheet to write down the negative assumptions that fuel your OCD, then refute them with corrective assumptions. Remember, assumptions are mini theories that apply to a variety of situations. Make sure the corrective assumptions refute the negative ones and give you new mini theories to help you when you feel overwhelmed by obsessive thoughts. Use the following worksheet as illustrated in the previous example to make positive changes in your assumptions.

OLD NEGATIVE ASSUMPTIONS	NEW CORRECTIVE ASSUMPTIONS

Just as you did with automatic thoughts, you can develop many obsession-reducing assumptions that will serve you better than those that trigger compulsive behaviors. If you're having trouble thinking of new assumptions to refute your old ones, review the example.

Of the new assumptions you've written, choose three that feel particularly true and comforting to you. Write them on an index card along with your corrective automatic thoughts. Carry the index card with you and review it often. Repetition is the way to transfer this new way of thinking about yourself into automatic thoughts; with additional repetition and experience, they will become your new assumptions.

Working on Your Core Beliefs

Core beliefs are broad generalizations about yourself and your place in the world. Core beliefs color the way you see yourself in a fundamental way that transcends situations. These beliefs can be negative or positive and predispose your emotional responses every day, all day long. When your core beliefs are positive, you feel good about yourself. The ones we're concerned about, however, are the negative ones. Negative core beliefs become activated when things are not going well. This is what happens when you obsess.

Negative core beliefs can include the assumption that you are a deeply damaged person or that you don't have what it takes to make use of any kind of help. These core beliefs keep you from believing that you can find relief from OCD. They set you up to have no hope. By understanding what your negative core beliefs are, you can challenge them and change them. The more often you catch yourself starting to believe them then refute those beliefs with a more accurate version of what's true about you, you create the conditions needed to allow your brain to change.

Here is a list of common negative core beliefs. Read them and see which one(s) feel true for you. Place an asterisk next to each one that you fear is true about you.

- I'm unlovable.
- I'm incompetent.
- I'm helpless.
- I'm undeserving.
- I'm powerless.
- I'm vulnerable.
- I'm bad/evil/wicked.
- I'm out of control/I'm crazy.
- I'm defective.
- I'm a failure.
- I'm weak.
- I'm needy.

Core beliefs generally form during childhood. The more dysfunctional your upbringing, the more deeply rooted your negative beliefs are likely to be. That means you may not initially be able to see that they are wrong. This might also be the case if you are depressed, victimized by domestic violence, are abusing alcohol or drugs, or are in other highly stressful circumstances. To loosen their hold on you, however, these beliefs need to be challenged.

Acting as though these negative beliefs are true is one way children protect themselves. They won't be overly disappointed if their expectations are low. Unless you've had a lot of positive corrective experiences as you grew up, these negative childhood beliefs are probably still active. If so, you continue to think these beliefs are true and try to use them to protect yourself from greater emotional (or physical) harm. If you don't think you deserve good things, you won't be surprised if you don't get them. If you think you're a bad person, it's not surprising that others are mean to you. This mechanism is a way to cope with your faulty negative core beliefs. Another way of dealing with your core beliefs is to confront them directly. Before we ask you to challenge the negative core belief(s) you identified on the previous page, let's begin assembling what you've worked on in this chapter.

Creating the Conditions to Allow Your Brain to Change

We've presented the idea that at the bottom of your anxiety and discomfort are one or more negative core beliefs. These core beliefs lead you to assume certain things are true about yourself and how the world works. In turn, those assumptions lead you to talk to yourself in predictable ways via negative automatic thoughts. Your actions are based on these beliefs and thoughts. In fact, your actions are an attempt to avoid or prevent bad things from happening. Being explicit about what you're trying to avoid or prevent is important to knowing how it relates to your thoughts and beliefs.

Let's look at an example of how all these concepts can come together to help you feel more in control of your OCD.

Alec Counts to Keep Anxiety in Check

Alec was an auditor who had become so fluid with numbers that they served as his second language. He began to think that everything had a numeric order. After a day at work in which he crunched numbers, he always made sure that he counted cars. During his commute, he counted blue cars, red cars, semitrucks, dump trucks, billboards, and numerous other objects. He counted them in groups of ten and then started again. He thought that the counting relaxed him. When for some reason he wasn't able to count he felt that something would go wrong.

One day, a colleague asked him for a ride home. On the drive, Alec attempted to count quietly under his breath while his coworker attempted to talk about the new organizational restructuring. Alec watched the traffic and counted as he listened to his coworker's concerns. When his colleague asked how he liked their new boss, Alec hesitated. He grew anxious while looking for enough trucks to get to ten before responding. As a "place marker" Alec suddenly said aloud, "8!" He saw the puzzled look on his colleague's face and realized that what he'd just said didn't make any sense to the man. Alec was embarrassed, then recovered and answered the question awkwardly.

After Alec dropped his coworker off, he couldn't shake the feeling that his count was wrong. He was sure if he didn't complete his ritual he wouldn't be able to relax at all that evening and probably not be able to get to sleep. The worst part was that he had the feeling that if something bad happened to his children, it would be his fault. He then drove all the way back to work so he could drive his usual route home while counting all the way. Alec clearly did not believe he was capable of tolerating the anxiety of not having counted everything properly.

ALEC'S ABC CHART

AUTOMATIC THOUGHTS	FEARED OUTCOMES	NEGATIVE ASSUMPTIONS	THINKING ERRORS	CORE BELIEFS	CORRECTIVE THOUGHTS
I can't take it if I don't drive back to work and count correctly.	Something bad will happen to my children.	My discomfort is linked to my children's safety.	Excessive responsibility Magical thinking Predicting the future Mistaking feelings for facts	I'm vulnerable. I'm weak.	My discomfort cannot harm my children. My feelings cannot predict the future. My discomfort is in my body; it doesn't impact events in the world.
	I won't be able to relax or sleep.	I can't tolerate anxiety.	Anxiety is intolerable.	I'm weak.	I can tolerate anxiety. Learning to tolerate anxiety will make me a stronger man.

As you can see from Alec's chart, there was more going on than a simple inability to tolerate the discomfort motivating his actions. By making clear, concrete connections between his automatic thoughts, his assumptions about how the world works, and his core beliefs, he gained insight into his behavior. Once he understood that his lifelong feelings of vulnerability and weakness were prompting him to act on faulty assumptions, he gained a degree of distance and objectivity. This enabled him to have greater clarity and motivation to get his OCD under control so that he could be a genuinely better father.

Now it's your turn to try to gain insight into your OCD. Fill in the chart below. Refer back to the automatic thoughts, thinking errors, assumptions, core beliefs, and corrective thoughts that you identified in the exercises earlier in this chapter.

Put it all together and make the connections clear between the different parts of your thoughts and beliefs. Pay particular attention to stating strong, simple, true corrective thoughts that can help you when that situation arises again.

ABC Chart

AUTOMATIC THOUGHTS	FEARED OUTCOMES	NEGATIVE ASSUMPTIONS	THINKING ERRORS	CORE BELIEFS	CORRECTIVE THOUGHTS

Refer back to this exercise and add to it as you encounter other automatic thoughts that you feel compelled to neutralize. What are the assumptions and core beliefs that form their foundation? What are the thinking errors that keep you from clearly examining your obsessive thinking and compulsive behaviors?

Remember, in order to allow your brain to change, you need to consistently challenge the thoughts and beliefs that maintain the present wiring. Your brain can and will change as long as you set up the proper conditions for it to do so. Writing these thoughts and linkages down is a proven way to take some of the power out of them and hand that power back to your logical, thinking brain. In the next chapter, we'll provide you with additional techniques you can use to allow your brain to change.

Chapter 6
The ABCs of Changing Your Behavior

In this chapter, we'll extend the work you did in the previous chapter and shift the emphasis to how you can allow your brain to change your behaviors. These elements will later be assembled into your individualized treatment plan for changing your obsessive thoughts and compulsive behaviors. We'll start by helping you identify the specific thoughts, images, and situations that trigger your OCD. Then you'll arrange those items into a table that will form the basis of your treatment plan that you'll complete in chapter 9. We'll give you examples along the way so you can see how this process has worked for others.

Identify Your Triggers

Although behaviors are more overt and easily identified, obsessive thoughts can be more difficult to catalog. Even though they are obsessive, people often overlook them because they are so familiar. In the case of mild OCD, obsessive thoughts may not seem so different from normal concerns. However, the fact is that these thoughts trigger the uncomfortable/anxious feelings that then lead to compulsive behaviors. Therefore, it's important to know what your triggers are.

In this section, we'll work together to create a summary of what most bothers you. We'll provide examples of how this is done, and then it will be your turn to do the exercises. Because cleaning and washing compulsions are so common, let's start there.

Example: Washing and Cleaning

Obsessions in this category generally have to do with concern for cleanliness and fear of germs or contamina-

tion. Although everyone can relate to a fear of coming into contact with germs, obsessive thoughts take it to extremes. In the mind of someone with OCD, germs take on extraordinary powers that defy all normal levels of protection and sanitation and travel from object to object, through the air, through barriers, only diminished in strength by the washing or cleaning ritual (or so it seems). But, of course, that's false. Just as germs don't have these feared magical qualities, washing and cleaning rituals are not so much about germs, disease, and health as they are about anxiety reduction. Rituals are an attempt to shut the gate that is stuck open in the striatum.

Somewhat different are obsessions with contamination. Often, concern with contamination is unrelated to germs or fear of disease. It's more related to the feeling of being dirty or having been in contact with something dirty, or sometimes just kind of an "icky" uncomfortable feeling. Here, too, the ability of suspected contaminants to travel is limited only by one's imagination. If a person can imagine a way that a contaminated object may have come into contact with other objects or mixed with them, then all are judged equally contaminated. The only way to avoid contamination is to avoid the millions of routes that the contamination might travel. Failing that, it's necessary to clean oneself to become decontaminated. This might also involve demanding that one's spouse and children clean themselves in ritualistic manners.

People with this particular affliction generally recognize that their desire for cleanliness is well beyond normal, but their logical mind is overruled by the obsession, which makes it very hard to think of anything else until the compulsive ritual is complete. One of the problems is that the ritual often gets more and more complex and takes longer and longer to complete. Let's look at an example to illustrate this point.

Lorraine's Story

Lorraine is a thirty-three-year-old single woman who works as a cashier in a supermarket. She initially came for treatment because she was afraid that she would lose her job if she didn't get OCD under control.

Lorraine's life had been difficult for the past six years because of OCD, but it became worse after her father died suddenly from a heart attack a year earlier. He had been a major source of comfort and support for her (and someone she relied on for reassurance when her OCD got bad). After the funeral she had a very difficult time returning to work. She had always been a bit bothered by handling raw packaged meat and now it was nearly intolerable. She developed a

method of putting a plastic bag over her hand to grab the package, then scanning it while getting it the rest of the way into the bag. That saved her from direct contact with the package and that worked for a while. Then she began noticing how frequently the conveyor was moist. She knew that many different items could wet it, such as the condensation from frozen items or jugs of milk, but she couldn't get it out of her mind that it was probably meat juice. To her, that represented contamination. If other items touched the moisture and she touched those groceries with an unprotected hand, she felt she too would be contaminated. She began to wear thin latex gloves and spray a cleaning product on the conveyor whenever it was wet and wipe it with paper towels. Then she got the idea that the latex gloves were no longer adequate prevention and the used paper towels in the trash can near her leg represented another threat of contamination.

At first she was able to wait for her scheduled breaks to dispose of the trash and wash her hands. Then she began taking more frequent breaks. Soon her compulsive behavior evolved. If her pants touched the trash can beneath her counter, they too were contaminated. Try as she might to avoid it, she sometimes brushed against it, or wondered whether she did and hadn't felt it. Soon, wondering whether she had touched the trash—and her inability to be certain that she hadn't—became the same as having touched it. That, of course, meant that she was in a near constant state of contamination. All she had to do was wonder whether she was contaminated and she rapidly became distracted and uncomfortable as she continued her work until break time. Sometimes on her break she would change her pants and put them into a plastic bag that she would seal. Then she washed her hands again to put on a fresh pair of pants before returning to work.

She later began obsessing about the fact that she put those plastic bags into a paper bag that she placed in the trunk of her car, which also became contaminated to her way of thinking. While her thoughts were spinning ever greater problems over a period of several weeks, her hand washing ritual grew in length and complexity until she was spending fifteen to thirty minutes at a time in the restroom. Fortunately, her coworkers began complaining of her long breaks and the manager threatened her with termination if she didn't get help.

To further complicate things, Lorraine also developed the idea that gasoline and gas fumes were contaminants, too. She felt that by touching the gas pump or the gas cap on her tank she then spread contamination to her car door handle, keys, and steering wheel. She developed another elaborate method of dealing with this source of contamination. It involved leaving her car door partially ajar, using latex gloves when touching the gas cap and pump, followed by disposing of the gloves and a quick cleansing with antimicrobial hand wipes in order to get back into the car without contaminating the interior.

At the root of her discomfort lay a particular fear. Lorraine had a very close relationship with her sister and they visited one another frequently. Lorraine was particularly haunted by the fear that if she were to hug or touch her four-year-old nephew, Jesse, she might transfer her contamination to him and he would get ill and die.

As part of her treatment, Lorraine wrote a brief summary of which situations or circumstances triggered her obsessive thoughts and how upsetting those thoughts were for her. The following shows how she summarized her situation.

LORRAINE'S OBSESSIVE THOUGHTS TRIGGER CHART OBSESSION: FEAR OF CONTAMINATION

TRIGGER SITUATION, THOUGHT, IMAGE	OBSESSIVE THOUGHTS/FEARED OUTCOME	SUD 1–100
Cashiering at work—I see a package of meat	Meat blood will get on me if I touch the package, even if it looks like the package is sealed.	50
Touching a package of meat	It's full of germs and now they're on my gloves. They'll multiply and get to my skin, and I'll get sick.	60–80
	Beef blood could have mad cow disease.	95
	Chicken blood is full of salmonella.	90
Arriving at work—I look at the cash register	My coworkers don't wash their hands often enough. They're dirty and it's dangerous to touch anything they've touched.	65
	Money is filthy.	45
Someone in line looks sick, or sneezes or coughs.	People's germs are all around me, I'm breathing them in, and they're getting on my face and skin.	50
My foot or leg bump against the trash basket.	Dirty paper towels are loaded with blood and germs. They'll get on me.	45
Going to my sister's house	If I touch Jesse with dirty hands he'll get sick.	80
	If Jesse dies it'll be my fault.	100
	My work clothes are contaminated.	50
Pumping gas	Gasoline and gas fumes are disgusting.	40
	I don't think latex gloves are adequate protection.	45
	I hate touching the gas cap—it's so dirty.	55
	Gas stations are filthy places. All kinds of people have touched the pumps.	55
	People stare at me and think I'm weird wearing gloves to pump gas.	60
	I think I might be crazy.	40
	I hope nobody reports me to the police.	35

Let's consider another example before it's your turn to create an Obsessive Thoughts Trigger Chart. This time, let's look at how someone who compulsively checks things might do it. Lucinda fears that some-thing bad will happen to her home while she's gone. She worries that it could get burglarized because she failed to lock the door, or that it might burn down if she neglects the stove or oven. Her chart is next.

LUCINDA'S OBSESSIVE THOUGHTS TRIGGER CHART OBSESSION: FEAR OF DISASTER

TRIGGER SITUATION, THOUGHT, OR IMAGE	OBSESSIVE THOUGHTS/FEARED OUTCOME	SUD 1–100
Seeing the stove before leaving the house in the morning	If it's on and I leave, the house will burn down.	80
Walking out of the house in the morning	If I don't lock it exactly right a burglar can get in.	60
After locking the house	I'm not sure I did it right; I'll just check one more time to be sure.	50
Going to bed at night	I better check the stove and oven just to be certain. Otherwise, I could kill us all.	65
Walking out of the kitchen after checking at night	I'll check one more time just to be certain.	45
Leaving the house in the morning before my husband	He might forget to unplug the toaster. I'll call him before he leaves.	60

YOUR OBSESSIVE THOUGHTS TRIGGERS

Now it's time to make your Obsessive Thoughts Trigger Chart. Start with the obsession that once under control will most improve your life. It doesn't have to be about germs or contamination. Whatever the theme of your obsession is, write it next to the word *obsession* on the following chart. Then identify the situations that are likely to activate it and briefly note the thoughts that bother you in that situation, followed by the associated SUD score. Just reflect on the past few days or weeks to get examples and write down the most common triggers.

This exercise can be uncomfortable for many people. This is especially true if you are worried about writing things down for fear that others might read them and learn what your thoughts

are. But the simple act of writing down your thoughts is part of treatment. It's frequently the case that writing can help loosen your obsession's hold on you. Writing thoughts makes them more defined and concrete. Sometimes people laugh at how ridiculous their thoughts are once they see them in black and white.

The people who have the most difficulty writing things down tend to be people with sexual and/or aggressive thoughts. These thoughts can be very disturbing and so far removed from any behavior that they would act on that the idea of committing them to paper is loaded with disgust and shame—it repels them. Some people fear that writing their thoughts down will make it more likely that they will act on them. Others are concerned that it could be used as evidence by police. These kinds of fears are examples of "thinking errors," which we discussed in the previous chapter.

If you have difficulty writing your thoughts in the chart below, we suggest that you write them on a separate sheet of paper and then shred or burn it once you finish. That way, you'll derive the benefit of writing down the thoughts and letting the more rational part of your brain process and assess them. Be sure to write them out the same way you would for the Obsessive Thoughts Trigger Chart below and to assign a SUD rating to your discomfort. This requires you to process the content of your thoughts as well as become aware of the intensity level of the feelings they generate. These are elements necessary for your brain to rewire itself. If you do feel that it's necessary to destroy your list, make a mental note of it so you can do additional work on it later.

Filling in this list is a big step toward regaining control of your life.

Obsessive Thoughts Trigger Chart

Obsession:

TRIGGER SITUATION, THOUGHT, OR IMAGE	OBSESSIVE THOUGHTS/FEARED OUTCOME	SUD 1–100

We'll do more work with this information in the next section, "Exposure Hierarchy." Therefore, it's important that you have a reasonably clear and well-defined picture of what is triggering your discomfort. So, if you feel your Obsessive Thoughts Trigger Chart is not complete, you might just try a bit harder right now to recall additional instances of your discomfort getting triggered. Certainly you have a wealth of experience to draw on for filling in this chart.

If your Obsessive Thoughts Trigger Chart seems reasonably complete, proceed to the next section. If your chart doesn't have very many entries and you feel stuck, try using the first principle of ORDER-ABC (which we'll discuss in the next chapter) the next time you become uncomfortable. "Observe" your thoughts. Note the circumstances that triggered your discomfort and the content of your thoughts. Why is it necessary for you to take action to neutralize your discomfort? Then return to your Obsessive Thoughts Trigger Chart and make additional entries. The better you are at documenting your triggers, the more accurate and efficient your treatment plan will be.

Too Anxious to Continue

Sometimes people are reluctant to do this exercise. Some are afraid of triggering their obsessive thoughts. Others might fear writing in the workbook or the possibility that others might see what they have written. We encourage you to put aside those fears for the moment and continue on with the exercise. It's essential to write things down to make what's going on in your mind as clear as you can. You might think you don't need to write down your thoughts because you're so familiar with them. The truth, however, is that you can take some of the power out of them by writing them down.

If you're feeling too anxious to continue, turn to the section "Relaxation" in chapter 10 (page 140) for relaxation techniques; and practice one or more before continuing with the writing exercise. But don't let your fears be an excuse to stop. Notice whether just thinking about how anxious you can get makes you anxious. When you're ready, add that to your list of triggers.

If you feel there is no way you could possibly write down your thoughts, that's a good indication that you should begin work with a licensed mental health clinician. It's important to find someone who is experienced in treating OCD. Refer back to the section on "Treatment Options" in chapter 3 (page 22) for how to choose a clinician to help you.

Exposure Hierarchy

In this section, you are going to rearrange your Obsessive Thoughts Trigger Chart into something that will be useful for your self-treatment program. As we mentioned earlier, the primary form of treatment for OCD is "exposure with response prevention," or ERP. We understand that exposure to your triggers can be extremely uncomfortable, so we're going to help you construct a treatment plan that will allow you to rewire your brain in a step-by-step fashion to achieve the maximum gain with the least discomfort. When your treatment plan is all done, you will determine which trigger you'll start with and how you'll progress to more difficult ones. That's why we need to start by converting your trigger chart into an exposure hierarchy. When you're finished, the ERP Hierarchy Chart will look like an ordered list of triggers—those with low SUD ratings at the top of the page, progressing to triggers with the highest SUD ratings at the bottom.

For example, Lorraine decided that her life would most dramatically improve if she could get her compulsive behavior at work under control. However, she wasn't willing to start there for fear of it not going well. So, Lorraine decided to work on her contamination obsession regarding pumping gas first. She arranged the items on her Obsessive Thoughts Trigger Chart in order of their SUD scores, from low to high, then identified the specific compulsive behavior she used to either avoid or neutralize each trigger.

LORRAINE'S OCD TRIGGER CHART

TRIGGER SITUATION, THOUGHT, OR IMAGE	OBSESSIVE THOUGHTS/FEARED OUTCOME	SUD 1–100	COMPULSION/RITUAL/ NEUTRALIZING BEHAVIOR
Pumping gas in gloves	I hope nobody reports me to the police.	35	Avoid eye contact.
Pumping gas in gloves	I think I might be crazy.	40	Avoid eye contact.
People seeing me pumping gas in gloves	People stare at me and think I'm weird wearing gloves to pump gas.	40	Avoid eye contact, be as quick as possible.
Smelling gas fumes	Gasoline and gas fumes are disgusting.	40	Hold breath while pumping gas.
Touching the gas pump	I don't think latex gloves are adequate protection.	55	Scrub hands with antimicrobial hand wash before getting back in car.
Unscrewing the gas cap	I hate touching the gas cap—it's so dirty.	60	Use gloves.
Touching the gas pump	Gas stations are filthy places. All kinds of people have touched the pumps.	70	Use gloves.
Hugging nephew	If I'm contaminated, he'll get it, too. He may become sick and die.	90	Avoid nephew until decontaminated.

After discussions with Lorraine, we devised a series of exposure situations that would help her overcome her fear of contamination by working through the Exposure Hierarchy. Because the first three items were somewhat related, we decided to lump them together as a single exposure. Lorraine's first task was to go to a gas station and, as she usually did, put her latex gloves on. With gloved hands she was to go inside the gas station and prepay for her gas and say to the clerk, "People probably think I'm crazy wearing these gloves to pump gas." Then wave and smile to anyone else pumping gas. Because the thought of waving to male strangers made her anxiety go up to 65 SUDs, we agreed she would only wave to women. Lorraine's completed Exposure Hierarchy is shown below, along with rules we devised for each exposure situation. You'll notice that the exposure rules are exactly the opposite of the behavior she used to "protect" herself from contamination and ultimately "protect" her nephew from his imagined death.

LORRAINE'S ERP HIERARCHY CHART

COMPULSIVE BEHAVIOR	SUD 1–100	EXPOSURE WITH RESPONSE PREVENTION RULES
Wearing latex gloves to pump gas while avoiding eye contact with other people	35–40	Wear gloves while saying to clerk, "People probably think I'm crazy wearing these gloves to pump gas." Smile and wave to other female patrons pumping gas.
Holding breath while touching gas pump	40	Breathe normally while handling gas pump.
Removing gloves before getting in car, then scrubbing hands with antimicrobial hand wash	55	Pump gas with gloves, then remove them and get in the car without using antimicrobial hand wash.
Wearing gloves through entire pumping procedure	60	Put gloves on after removing gas cap and take gloves off after pumping but before putting gas cap back on.
Wearing gloves when touching gas pump	70	Pump gas without wearing gloves.
Avoiding hugging nephew unless fully decontaminated	90	Drive from gas station to sister's home and hug nephew.

By starting with an exposure in the 35 to 40 SUD range, Lorraine felt confident she could do it. We agreed that she would continue to do this specific exposure until it no longer provoked discomfort greater than 30. Once that was completed, she continued on as quickly as possible to the next exposure and repeated it until her discomfort with that task was minimal. In order to be able to do multiple exposures in succession, Lorraine only purchased small amounts of gasoline at various gas stations.

Lorraine quickly met with success on her first outing. When she said, "People probably think I'm crazy to wear gloves when I pump gas," the attendant chuckled and said, "You've got no idea how many people come in here with those on." Lorraine reported an immediate sense of relief, realizing that her fear of being taken away by the police was silly. Waving and smiling came easily after that. She finished her gas purchase with the remainder of her rituals in place.

Leaving that station, she immediately went to another and repeated her performance. This time, her distress level was much reduced, though she reported being annoyed by the need to do the rest of her rituals in exchange for so little gasoline. She went directly to a third gas station and, noting little discomfort, decided to move on to the second exposure of not holding her breath while pumping gas. Lorraine allocated ninety minutes to her exposure exercises. On the first day, she comfortably accomplished the first two items on her Exposure Hierarchy Chart. She also managed to avoid scrubbing her hands at two gas stations, though she did not achieve complete relief from this trigger until her next exposure session.

Over a three-week period, Lorraine went on seven of these outings, each approximately ninety minutes long. With each session her confidence grew as she conquered her fears. By the seventh outing she was simultaneously eager and anxious. She had kept her sister abreast of her progress, as she was one of Lorraine's two support people (the other being Lorraine's boyfriend). Arriving at her sister's home after pumping gas without gloves, Lorraine was hesitant to touch her

nephew. Her sister stood silently by giving no reassurance beyond her presence and previous agreement to the treatment plan. Lorraine's moment of caution was overcome by her nephew's exuberant wrapping his arms around her legs by way of greeting. Lorraine reported that experience was like diving into a pool of cold water. Over the next hour and a half, Aunt Lorraine continued to come and go, dispensing hugs only to get back into her car and return moments later with slightly more gas in her tank.

Approximately two weeks into these seven sessions, Lorraine's confidence and relief were great enough that she began simultaneously working on a separate ERP Hierarchy Chart for her workplace. At the conclusion of the seventh gas pump desensitizing session followed by hugging her nephew, her progress at the supermarket proceeded rapidly because she had already faced her greatest fear, contaminating her nephew.

Hopefully, this example has given you a graphic understanding of how ERP works and how it builds on each previous success. Succeeding at a relatively easy task makes the next one a bit easier. Each step continues to be challenging, but not overwhelmingly so. The key to this method's success is constructing an exposure hierarchy that's custom made for you. That requires specific information about your obsessive triggers and compulsive behaviors. Time, thought, and tolerating some unpleasant feelings need to go into the development of the hierarchy.

Your support person can be of great help in this task because you might not be fully aware of how clever you've been at avoiding your triggers and neutralizing them. (Lorraine, for instance, frequently asked her boyfriend to fill her car with gas to save her the trouble and discomfort. In order for her to improve she agreed to stop asking him for this kind of "help.") Your support person will probably also be very helpful in thinking of exposure situations, because before you have worked through your hierarchy it will be difficult for you to imagine doing the things you most want to avoid.

YOUR ERP HIERARCHY CHART

The ERP Hierarchy Chart, opposite page, when finished, will be a complete accounting of the various ways your obsession gets triggered and the compulsive behaviors you engage in to neutralize your discomfort.

Start your hierarchy by transferring items from your Obsessive Thoughts Trigger Chart that have SUD ratings no lower than 40. Most people find that something around that level is a good place to begin. It's a bit uncomfortable, but not so difficult that you can't imagine yourself doing the exposure. Start with something you are confident you'll succeed at. We want you to get a feeling for ERP while at the same time beginning the process of rewiring your brain. Triggers with SUD ratings lower than 40 will automatically resolve themselves as you work on items with higher discomfort ratings.

Once you've transferred all the Trigger Situations, Obsessive Thoughts, and SUD information and have ranked them from low SUD to high, you're ready for the next step. Now, identify the compulsive behaviors that you use to neutralize your discomfort for each trigger, just as Lorraine did. Write that in the last column of the chart. In addition to overt behaviors, don't forget to include avoidance of the situation as one of the ways you manage it, as well as thought rituals. This is another big step toward freeing yourself of OCD.

ERP Hierarchy Chart

TRIGGER SITUATION, THOUGHT, OR IMAGE	OBSESSIVE THOUGHTS/FEARED OUTCOME	SUD 1–100	COMPULSION/RITUAL/NEUTRALIZING BEHAVIOR

In the next chapter we're going to give you additional examples designed to deal with other types of obsessions. These examples will help you get more familiar with how ERP treatment is conducted before you construct your treatment plan.

ERP Specifics

Now that you have a better understanding of what ERP is and how it can be applied to help you get better, let's have a closer look at why it works. This will help solidify your understanding as to why you need to tolerate some discomfort. Once you get started on your own exposure hierarchy, there will be times you will need to remind yourself why you're doing what you're doing and why you need to persist.

Exposure with Response Prevention

Effective OCD treatment needs to include "exposure with response prevention." Exposure means intentionally exposing yourself to something that will trigger your obsessive thoughts. "Response prevention" means not engaging in your compulsive behavior afterward.

You have probably tried many times not to engage in your compulsive behaviors. But it's less likely that you have intentionally tried to trigger your obsessive thoughts. If you're like most people with OCD, you've worked hard to limit your obsessive thinking. It's common for people to try avoiding situations that will trigger them, or once such thoughts begin to try and distract yourself, attempt to change your thoughts, or stop them in some way as soon as you can. When all else fails, you use your compulsive ritual to terminate the obsession and the anxious/uncomfortable feelings that go along with it.

So, a big difference between therapy and what you've been doing up until now is that you're going to take control of the OCD. You take control by having it happen on your terms. You allow it to occur so you can achieve a very specific goal: rewiring your brain and terminating OCD. Most people with OCD are frightened by this idea. This is probably a new idea to you. The fact is, however, it's an essential element of the most highly effective treatment.

Let's talk a bit more about the process of exposure with response prevention so you get more comfortable with how and why it works. This technique has been proven to work whether your trigger is a specific situation, an object, or a thought. It works because we make use of how the brain learns and apply those principles to re-educating the parts that are causing the OCD. Some of the main principles involved are:

Neurons that fire together wire together. This statement summarizes a great deal about how we learn both explicit information, such as the name and phone number of a new friend, and more automatic kinds of responses, such as what makes us uncomfortable or fearful. The more we do something, the stronger those brain circuits become. For example, the more a person practices playing the guitar, the more ingrained those connections become and the quicker the fingers respond to the thought of playing a particular note or chord. Similarly, the more a person thinks a particular thought (e.g., "I'm contaminated") and responds with a specific behavior (e.g., take a shower), the stronger the link between those two things becomes.

When repetition is combined with the fact that the parts of the brain that serve as a "thermostat" are overly active in OCD, you get a very tightly wired circuit. It's a circuit that isn't working properly, but it is reliable, consistent, and difficult to reprogram. It is especially hard to reprogram if you apply the wrong methods, or you use the right methods but do so inconsistently. So what is the right method? The answer: exposure with response prevention.

How does ERP undo that OCD wiring? That brings us to the next important principle: **habituation**. "Habituation" is a word psychologists use that roughly means brain circuits stop firing in the old way because they get tired of being ignored. They responded as they were wired to respond, but then no one paid attention, so they finally reach a limit and stop. An example of this might be walking into a friend's house that has an unpleasant odor, perhaps from cigarettes or something being cooked that you don't enjoy. At first, the smell is quite strong, but within a few minutes it becomes imperceptible. The brain's olfactory center alerts you to the fact that there is a disagreeable odor, but then stops signaling after having its information ignored during your continued exposure.

The next principle is **extinction**. This refers to the connections between different parts of a circuit getting weaker and weaker until they are only mildly wired together. This happens because "neurons that stop firing together stop being wired together." This is our goal in ERP. We want the trigger situation to stop initiating obsessive thoughts, and your anxiety reduction to become disconnected from the compulsive behaviors.

Additionally, we want new learning to take place. We want you to get used to those old rigid OCD circuits not getting triggered. We want you to get used to having a choice of how to respond. Then on the rare occasion your anxiety does get reactivated, you can easily "remind" yourself that you have a choice and then do what you want to do, not what OCD used to force you to do.

Exposure with response prevention extinguishes OCD circuits once you've tolerated your obsessive thoughts and resisted the compulsive behavior frequently enough and long enough that the anxiety dies down. However, ERP must be done consistently so that the OCD circuits repeatedly get the same message that they are no longer needed. Then, and only then, does your brain become fully rewired.

In summary, the essential ingredients of ERP are:

1. Exposing yourself to one of your triggers, voluntarily

2. Observing and tolerating the discomfort generated by your obsessive thoughts

3. Resisting the ritual by not engaging in the old compulsive behavior

4. Doing something new and interesting, instead of ritualizing

5. Allowing your brain to take it all in so it can make the needed changes

6. Persisting until your discomfort subsides or you need to do something else

In practice, this therapeutic method is applied systematically and gradually. You begin with the less difficult triggers and work up to the more difficult ones. This allows new circuits to gain strength while the old ones fall into disuse and you gain confidence in the procedure. This therapeutic method can set you free. It has worked for thousands of people suffering from OCD. It can work for you, too.

Depending on how severe your OCD is, this undertaking could be a very challenging one. But if your OCD is moderate to severe, you are going to be highly anxious no matter what choice you make. It will occur intrusively, against your will, with no prospect of improvement, or by your own choice with the very real prospect of getting better.

In the next chapter, you'll learn a method that will put together everything you have learned so far to help you ease into making the fundamental changes needed to put OCD behind you.

Chapter 7

Putting It Together with ORDER-ABC

OCD is considered a psychiatric disorder. That means your brain is not functioning properly. We want to help you get your life back in good, healthy, comfortable working condition. To do so, your brain needs to be rewired so it is no longer disordered. We have created an acronym to help you remember the steps to take when you're having trouble. The acronym is ORDER-ABC. We previously mentioned that ABC stands for "Allow your Brain to Change." In essence, your job is to create the conditions that make it possible for your brain to do its job and change for the better. The ORDER acronym will help you remember what those conditions are. We'll discuss each aspect of the acronym in detail, but let's start with an overview of what the letters stand for:

O—Observe—Instead of struggling to push obsessive thoughts out of your awareness, or neutralize them with compulsive behaviors, you are going develop your ability to watch your thoughts. You will become more mindful of what you are thinking, and you will learn to see OCD thoughts for what they are: thoughts that you don't like or want flooding your conscious awareness. By increasing your ability to observe your thoughts, you will help yourself detach from your OCD pattern, as if you were just an observer of it, instead of someone feeling the pain.

R—Remind—By reminding yourself that the thoughts you are having are OCD, you will engage the parts of your brain that know OCD is not the real you. You will remind yourself that your brain is not thinking clearly, that the striatum's gate is stuck open, that a flood of obsessive thoughts and compulsive behaviors is a problem you are working to fix. Reminding pulls the covers off OCD thoughts and keeps you aware of what they are.

D—Do Something Different—Doing something other than your usual OCD compulsive behaviors helps extinguish the old wiring and at the same time establishes new wiring. The absolute best thing to do is described by the next two letters of our acronym.

E—Exposure—This is the "E" of the ERP technique that you learned about in the last chapter. This involves confronting the situations, thoughts, and images that provoke your OCD. We'll teach you how to do this in a controlled, gradual, step-by-step fashion.

R—Response Prevention—This means refraining from compulsive behaviors that *seem* to make you feel better but in reality keep you locked into OCD. We'll help you make a specific plan involving this key technique to break out of your OCD.

And finally:

ABC—Allow your Brain to Change. The steps above are what you need to do to set up the conditions for your brain to do what it wants to do, rewire itself in a way that leads to healthy, optimal functioning.

Putting real ORDER back into your life requires taking all of these steps together and doing them over and over. Each time you do so, your old OCD circuits will extinguish a little bit more and new, more useful and relaxed circuits will grow stronger. Let's take a closer look at what's involved.

Observing

One of the principal features of OCD is a deeply entrenched obsessive thought pattern. These are generally so uncomfortable that your natural inclination to terminate the thoughts by whatever means possible overrides your ability to challenge the thoughts. This sets you on the path of reinforcing the OCD cycle and making your thoughts and behaviors more tightly bound together.

You need a way to get your attention out of the automatic OCD habit. One of the best ways to do this is to observe your obsessional pattern by paying attention to what you're thinking and doing as if you're watching another person. By paying attention to how you are obsessing and compulsively behaving, you shine a spotlight on your automatic obsessive thoughts and compulsive behaviors. You essentially interrupt the OCD cycle, which has become a terrible bad habit.

Thus, the first step in breaking a habit is to pay attention. For example, when riding a bicycle, as soon as you think too much about how you are pedaling or keeping your balance, you start to wobble. You interrupt the habit, as if to cast doubt on it.

Observing also allows you to be a "critic" of your own behavior. Instead of mindlessly going from one obsessive thought to another, you stand back and observe yourself and say, "Hey, wait a minute! What am I doing?" This also affords you an opportunity to determine whether your obsessive thoughts are realistic. You implicitly ask: "Are these concerns realistic?" This is because you've widened your perspective by taking a step back to a stance of watching your thoughts rather than being completely enmeshed with them. Because OCD breeds a narrowness in thinking and a locked-in brain pattern, the initial step of observing will help you enlarge your perspective.

Attention also helps you rewire your brain, because as you focus, you engage your frontal lobes. As we explained in chapter 4, your frontal lobes are a kind of brain within a brain, the executive brain. They influence the use of resources and activity in other parts of your brain. They "decide" what to do and where to invest your energies. The first step in activating your frontal lobes is paying attention, which involves observation.

There is a meditation technique called "mindfulness" that can help you become an observer. Although we will describe mindfulness in more detail in chapter 8 (page 100), the basic concept is that by being completely present in the here and now instead of worrying about and anticipating the future, you free yourself from the anxiety that underlies your OCD. As you become mindfully present, you detach from your obsessions about what might happen in the future. You also free your mind to realistically appraise your current situation. You ask yourself whether you are really in need of repeating the same compulsive behaviors. By being mindfully observant of the present, you put real ORDER back into your life by detaching from the mindlessness of OCD.

The first step in ORDER-ABC is learning to observe, and the following exercise will help you practice this, which will also set up the conditions for the rest of the steps. This is why practicing this initial step is so important. Using the following worksheet, observe your thoughts and make a quick note as to what you're thinking. For the next five minutes, simply become the watcher of your thoughts. Make a brief notation every thirty seconds as to what you're thinking about—just a word or two is sufficient—then resume watching the flow of your thoughts. For example, you might just jot down things such as: "I want to keep reading," "Thinking about food," "Feeling like I'm wasting my time," "Blank, just staring," "Noticing my heartbeat," "Worrying about problem at work," "Worrying someone will interrupt me," "Afraid if I don't control my thoughts, obsessive thoughts will start," or "Feeling unusually peaceful." This exercise will help you become more aware of your inner stream of consciousness.

OBSERVATIONS
0.5 minutes
1.0 minutes
1.5 minutes
2.0 minutes
2.5 minutes
3.0 minutes
3.5 minutes
4.0 minutes
4.5 minutes
5.0 minutes

This exercise sounds simple, but if you're like most people, it was more difficult than you thought it would be. It's challenging to disengage from our thoughts. Most people get lost in their thoughts and have to "snap out of it" in order to jot them down. This is a skill that takes some practice, and we encourage you to do this exercise each day. As you might imagine, there is a part of the brain that gets strengthened by practicing this exercise. The stronger it gets, the better equipped you'll be to shut that striatal gate when it gets stuck open.

Reminding

The reminding step requires that you remind yourself that your thinking and behaviors are simply *obsessional* thinking and *compulsive* behaviors. When you find yourself obsessing, you can say, "I must not forget that this is my brain acting out its OCD. My striatum is not doing its job of filtering out nuisance information like it should be."

The reminding step activates your hippocampus, which as you learned earlier is a critical part of your memory system. Your hippocampus, along with your orbital frontal cortex, helps tame your amygdala. It says, in effect, "Hey, calm down! There's nothing to get excited about."

Reminding yourself to label OCD for what it is helps you activate your left frontal lobe. Your left frontal lobe uses language to label what is going on at any one time, while it also generates positive feelings. By reminding yourself that it's your OCD that's making you uncomfortable, you stimulate your left frontal lobe to lower your anxiety and thereby the fuel for OCD.

Reminding yourself to label your obsessive thoughts as exactly what they are—OCD—helps you shift from obsessional thinking to realistic thinking. For example, not wanting to leave your house in the morning until you've said the number seven to yourself seven times is not going to make your day go better. It's OCD! Showering your body in an exact sequence is not about hygiene. It's OCD! Checking the news to make sure you didn't hit someone with your car and unintentionally kill him or her is not being a concerned citizen. It's OCD! Asking your spouse (for the tenth time) whether she thinks the spot on your arm is cancerous is not a health question. It's OCD!

Reminding yourself to label your obsessions and compulsions as symptoms of OCD exercises your rational thought process. It also rewires your brain because it strengthens the connections between your frontal lobes and parts of your brain such as your amygdala that have been overactivated. In a sense, labeling provides the striatum with training wheels so that it can start filtering nuisance thoughts and therefore closing the gate so you can move on to thinking about something else. The result? You won't suffer as much from OCD.

REMINDING WORKSHEET

This exercise for the reminding step will help you practice how labeling shifts you away from the locked-in OCD brain loop. In the following worksheet, write down ten statements you can say to yourself when your OCD acts up. Write down whatever comes to mind. These remarks will help remind you that what you are experiencing is not reality, it's OCD.

REMINDING YOURSELF TO LABEL YOUR OCD SYMPTOMS	
1.	6.
2.	7.
3.	8.
4.	9.
5.	10.

Once you have ten statements, read back over them and asterisk the five that make you feel calmer when you read them to yourself. Read them repeatedly and commit them to memory. This stores them in your hippocampus. Now when you want to calm yourself, remind yourself to say these phrases. In turn, they will help deactivate your anxiety-generating amygdala and get your striatum unstuck. Don't neglect to commit these to memory. When you're under attack from OCD, you'll need them. They can help you, so don't shortchange yourself. Study the five phrases that give you the greatest sense of calm.

Doing

Doing something different than what you have compulsively done in the past is critical. There are two main methods we want you to use. The first method is what you will do when you're following the treatment plan that you will make for yourself in chapter 9. What you do differently will follow some rules you'll define for yourself (with our help). This will include exposure with response prevention while paying attention and observing how you're feeling and noticing how that changes during your self-treatment session. When using this method, the more you pay attention to your discomfort, the quicker it will dissipate and the more quickly your brain will change.

The second method can be used when you're not doing one of your "formal" or planned treatment sessions. This approach has a few variations, but it is essentially a delay technique. For example, imagine you're at work or school and begin to obsess about something "dirty" you touched. In this case, the "do something different" has a wide range of possible actions. What we don't want you to do is immediately give in to your compulsive desire to wash. We want you to delay for as long as you can. Instead of washing your hands, check your email, talk with a friend or coworker, make a phone call, or tell yourself you'll wash but not for another ten or fifteen minutes. Delay the urge as long as you can.

If you're at home, take a walk, do a chore that needs doing, talk with a family member, listen to music, read the paper, pay some bills, do an errand, or start a pleasurable activity. Here, too, make a deal with yourself that you'll do your compulsion, but not for another five, ten, or fifteen minutes. At the end of that time, make another deal to wait an additional five or ten minutes. Delay as long as possible. The key here is to engage in this different behavior so you interrupt the automatic relationship between your obsessive thoughts and the compulsive behavior and do it long enough that your discomfort begins to subside. After practicing this technique consistently, you'll find it easier and easier.

For people with mild OCD, this delay technique may be all you need to make a huge difference in your OCD. You may find that consistent practice of delaying is sufficient for you to "forget" your need to ritualize. This can be particularly effective if you engage in an activity that is highly enjoyable or interesting. So think of a few activities that you like and list them in the following worksheet. Identify a few things to choose from at home, work, school, or other places you frequent. If you're in a position to do one when your compulsive urge strikes—do it! If you have a favorite diversion on your computer or cell phone, be sure to list it.

ENJOYABLE ACTIVITIES LIST	
1.	6.
2.	7.
3.	8.
4.	9.
5.	10.

Another version of this method is that once you begin your compulsion, do *it* differently. Modify it in some way. Change it any way you can think to do so. Remember, you're trying to interrupt the brain circuitry that maintains these automatic behaviors. So throw a monkey wrench in there. Sing while you do your ritual, talk aloud to yourself, stand on one foot, or use your nondominant hand. Similarly, change your mental images from people to cartoons, dangerous objects to things made out of Play-Doh, your inner pictures of people being harmed to images of people bouncing back up, brushing themselves off, and saying something silly like, "Ah, that was refreshing." The sillier you make things, the better. It helps to loosen your very rigid,

overly serious, obsessive-compulsive wiring. This will almost certainly be difficult for you to do. Hang in there with it. With practice, you'll get better at it and you'll be rewarded with less intense discomfort.

List a number of possible images or actions in the next worksheet. It's far better to think about this now and suggest some options while you're calm than try to come up with things when you're feeling anxious and uncomfortable. We are not very creative or clever when we're feeling bad. So take a few minutes and make a list of possible changes you could make to your most common obsessive thoughts and compulsive behaviors. Remember the sillier, the better.

MODIFIED/SILLY ACTIONS AND IMAGES LIST	
1.	6.
2.	7.
3.	8.
4.	9.
5.	10.

Escape clause: If, after introducing some type of change to your obsessive thought or compulsive behavior and persisting with it for a few minutes (or more), you continue to feel you must redo your compulsion according to your ritual—go ahead and do it the way you feel you must. But the next time introduce some form of change or silliness again. Preferably, you'll use a new and different modification to keep your change from turning into part of your ritual. Give it a try; loosen up those circuits!

Exposure

Exposure means exposing yourself to what you fear so that the anxiety associated with that fear can fade away. Exposure is a basic principle in anxiety treatment, as we emphasized in the last chapter. It is the "E" in ERP. Exposure is the opposite of avoidance, which along with "escape" are the worst things you can do because they maintain the anxious brain circuits underlying OCD. Avoidance means that you do things to avoid feeling anxious. For example, you might avoid shaking hands with someone so that you don't feel compelled to wash, or avoid being the last one out of the house so you don't have to get caught up in wondering whether you locked the door properly. Your compulsive behaviors, on the other hand, are the primary way you escape from feeling anxious. Avoidant and escape behaviors are short-term fixes that perpetuate your long-term problem—namely, OCD.

The primitive part of your brain that responds to anxiety and discomfort doesn't know that these are short-term solutions that don't work in the long term. That part of your brain thinks they work just fine. So every time you engage in avoidance and escape, you strengthen those brain circuits. For example, you use a public restroom and worry the rest of the day that you may have gotten germs from the toilet seat. You shower as soon as you get home and then feel more relaxed. This is not about hygiene—it's a form of escape. You escape the anxiety of your irrational fear by showering. Your primitive brain notices you feel better now, so it figures showering is the correct solution to the problem. That part of your brain doesn't know the real problem is OCD. So the next time you use a public restroom you think you know what the solution is—shower. So you need to remind yourself what the real problem is and then act in a way that will fix it. The only way that you'll be able to rewire the old habit into a new habit is by intentionally exposing yourself to the situation that you find anxiety provoking and not using your neutralizing behavior (to solve the wrong problem).

By exposing yourself to your trigger situations, you make the critical step toward taming your OCD. Recall from chapter 4 that there is no quick fix for calming your amygdala. You'll need to habituate yourself to the anxiety-provoking situation by consistent exposure. In other words, by exposing yourself over and over to knowing that your hands were washed only once and finding that you don't die of a terrible infection, eventually your amygdala will dampen its overreactivity.

During your exposure, use realistic, positive self-talk. This helps your cortex (the higher part of your brain) tell your amygdala (the lower part of your brain) that there's nothing to get anxious about. For example, say, "Each time I don't wash my hands more than once nothing bad happens. The world is full of people who wash their hands normally and they don't drop dead." By activating your cortex in this way, you promote stronger downward connections from your frontal lobes to your amygdala. You do this with reassuring, positive self-talk.

Exposure is an absolutely critical part of the ORDER-ABC method. It implies voluntarily initiating your OCD for the purpose of getting it under control. For maximum effect, it also involves being attentive to what you're doing without trying to distract yourself from the uncomfortable feelings that get generated. In the next chapter, we'll review a number of specific ways to use exposure to reduce your OCD.

Response Prevention

Response prevention is another key part of the treatment of OCD. It follows immediately after the exposure step. As we described in the previous chapter, combined with exposure this is referred to as Exposure with Response Prevention, or ERP for short.

Researchers agree that response prevention works as long as you feel some anxiety when you don't engage in the old behavior. That's right, feel some anxiety! This may be a frightening thought, and you may think that we aim to torture you. But the fact is, by *not doing* your old compulsive behavior during the exposure phase you are doing the most important work to tame your amygdala. This is where habituation really occurs.

Most OCD therapists recommend that each ERP session last at least forty-five to ninety minutes. During that time you allow yourself to feel the uncomfortable feelings while *not* engaging in your old compulsive behavior. This gives the primitive part of your brain, as well as your cortex, a chance to learn that nothing bad happens when you don't use your neutralizing ritual. By hanging in there and not engaging in the old compulsive behaviors—you give your brain time to rewire itself.

Chapter 8

Practice Making ORDER-ABC Treatment Plans

n this chapter, we'll provide you with sample ERP treatment plans for the most common types of OCD. This will give you an opportunity to see how others have succeeded in treatment as well as give you a chance to practice developing ERP treatment rules. To get the most out of this chapter it's important that you work the examples. By doing these exercises, you'll develop the ability to think about your own situation and create an effective treatment plan for yourself in the next chapter.

On the one hand, ERP is simple. It pretty much just boils down to "stop doing that!" However, as you know, it isn't that easy. That's why we want you to stop your compulsive behaviors in a step-by-step fashion just as Lorraine did. It gets a bit tricky to set things up so that you stop doing some things but not others when they all make you uncomfortable. That's the power of creating and using the ERP Hierarchy Chart (that you made for yourself in chapter 6). You'll work your way, a step at a time, from moderately uncomfortable exposures to the things that bother you most.

But first, review all the treatment plans provided in this section. The exercises will help you to think like an ERP therapist. You'll get to practice writing ERP rules for others. This will be an excellent way for you to get comfortable with the logic of ERP. Then when you work on your own plan, which is likely to make you nervous to think about, you'll be well prepared to create rules that will really work.

Contamination, Avoidance, and Washing

n chapter 6 we saw how Lorraine got control of her fear of contamination while pumping gas. But let's have a closer look at how she worked with her contamination fear and excessive hand washing at work. The chart below is her ERP Treatment Hierarchy Chart. Read each line. Consider the trigger, her thoughts about it, the SUD rating, and the compulsive behavior she uses to neutralize her discomfort. Then write the ERP rules that you think will work. Each box in the "Exposure Rules" and "Response Prevention Rules" columns contains a letter corresponding to additional space after the chart in which you can write your thoughts.

Write the rules in a way that expose Lorraine to the specific trigger listed on that line. Then write a rule that prevents her from using her compulsive behavior to neutralize the discomfort. At the same time, the rule should allow her to neutralize the next higher trigger on the hierarchy if she doesn't want to push herself to overcome more than one trigger at a time. (This sounds more complex than it is. Once you start working the example, you'll get the hang of it.) Remember, not all exposures need to happen on the same day and you can give her some exposures at home in preparation for encountering a trigger at work.

Complete one trigger at a time, compare your answer with Lorraine's on the next page, and then move on to the next trigger, incorporating what you just learned. Try not to read ahead. Don't worry if you don't get it "right." The chances are it will take some practice before you start to think in terms of ERP rules. The most important thing is for you to try to

figure it out and then see what Lorraine did. Not knowing and struggling to come up with a workable plan is an important part of the learning process. Don't cheat yourself out of learning. Take your time and decide what you think would make effective rules. Doing these sample charts with your support person would be an excellent way for both of you to gain the skill to do this successfully for the most important person . . . you.

LORRAINE'S ERP TREATMENT HIERARCHY CHART

TRIGGER SITUATION, THOUGHT, OR IMAGE	AUTOMATIC THOUGHTS	SUD 1–100	COMPULSION/RITUAL/NEUTRALIZING BEHAVIOR	EXPOSURE RULES	RESPONSE PREVENTION RULES
Getting my cash drawer at the office and handling money all day long	Money is filthy. I'll get contaminated if it touches my skin.	45	Put latex gloves on before getting cash drawer. Wear gloves all day long.	A	A
My foot or leg bumping against the trash basket	Dirty paper towels are loaded with blood and germs. They'll get me.	45	Put trash basket under counter as far from me as possible. Push towels down with gloved hand so they don't stick up and touch me.	B	B
Someone in line looking sick, or sneezing or coughing	People's germs are all around me; I'm breathing them in, and they're getting on my face and skin.	50	Hold my breath and turn away when someone coughs or sneezes. Exhale out mouth, then nose to blow germs away before inhaling.	C	C
Cashiering at work—I see a package of meat	Meat blood will get on me if I touch the package, even if it looks like the package is sealed.	50	Check other items first, leave it until last.	D	D

(continued on page 90)

TRIGGER SITUATION, THOUGHT, OR IMAGE	AUTOMATIC THOUGHTS	SUD 1–100	COMPULSION/RITUAL/NEUTRALIZING BEHAVIOR	EXPOSURE RULES	RESPONSE PREVENTION RULES
Arriving at work—I look at the cash register	My coworkers don't wash their hands often enough. They're dirty from touching money and it's dangerous to touch anything they've touched.	65	Put cash drawer in with gloved hands. If no one's in line, spray register with cleaner and wipe with paper towels. If someone's in line, only use the tip of my index finger to touch the register buttons, then spray and wipe it as soon as possible.	E	E
Touching a package of fish	Fish are icky, stinky, and full of germs, and now those germs are on my gloves. They'll multiply and get to my skin, and I'll get sick.	70–80	Put plastic bag over my left hand, grab item, and pull bag up and over it with my right hand. Wash hands on break.	F	F
Touching a package of chicken	Chicken blood is full of salmonella. It could kill me.	90	Put plastic bag over my left hand, grab item, and pull bag up and over it with my right hand. Ask for break if I get too anxious. Wash hands on break until I feel clean. Sometimes that takes ten minutes with hot water and a lot of soap.	G	G
Touching a package of beef	Beef blood could have mad cow disease. It could kill me.	95	Put plastic bag over my left hand, grab item, and pull bag up and over it with my right hand. Ask for break if I get too anxious. Wash hands on break until I feel clean. Sometimes that takes ten minutes with hot water and a lot of soap.	H	H
Being near my nephew after work without showering first	I'm contaminated. He'll get it too and get sick and die.	100	Go home and shower before visiting. If I need to drop something off, leave it on porch, then call on cell phone after I'm in the car again.	I	I

Write the ERP rules that you think Lorraine could use.

A. Exposure Rules:

B. Exposure Rules:

C. Exposure Rules:

D. Exposure Rules:

E. Exposure Rules

F. Exposure Rules:

G. Exposure Rules:

A. Response Prevention Rules:

B. Response Prevention Rules:

C. Response Prevention Rules:

D. Response Prevention Rules:

E. Response Prevention Rules:

F. Response Prevention Rules:

G. Response Prevention Rules:

(continued on page 92)

H. Exposure Rules:

- -

- -

I. Exposure Rules:

- -

- -

H. Response Prevention Rules:

- -

- -

I. Response Prevention Rules:

- -

- -

LORRAINE'S ERP TREATMENT HIERARCHY CHART

TRIGGER SITUATION, THOUGHT OR IMAGE	AUTOMATIC THOUGHTS	SUD 1–100	COMPULSION/RITUAL/ NEUTRALIZING BEHAVIOR	EXPOSURE RULES	RESPONSE PREVENTION RULES
Getting my cash drawer at the office and handling money all day long	Money is filthy. I'll get contaminated if it touches my skin.	45	Put latex gloves on before getting cash drawer. Wear gloves all day long.	1. One hour before needing to leave for work, take dollar bill from wallet and rub it with both hands. Touch it against my arms, legs, face, hair, and clothes. Wait until anxiety subsides. 2. Go to work and get cash drawer without gloves on.	1. Don't wash hands after money exposure. Don't change clothes. Go to work. 2. At cash register, put gloves on after inserting cash drawer. Gloves are needed to prevent premature exposure to triggers with higher SUDs.
My foot or leg bumping against the trash basket	Dirty paper towels are loaded with blood and germs. They'll get me.	45	Put trash basket under counter as far from me as possible. Push towels down with gloved hand so they don't stick up and touch me.	1. Resist the urge to wipe the counter with cleaning spray and paper towels. 2. If I wipe the counter, touch the used paper towel against both arms, body, and both legs before putting it in the trash.	1. Don't take extra pants to work or change clothes during my break. 2. Hands may have gloves on to avoid touching meat packages.

TRIGGER SITUATION, THOUGHT OR IMAGE	AUTOMATIC THOUGHTS	SUD 1–100	COMPULSION/RITUAL/ NEUTRALIZING BEHAVIOR	EXPOSURE RULES	RESPONSE PREVENTION RULES
Someone in line looking sick, or sneezing or coughing	People's germs are all around me; I'm breathing them in, and they're getting on my face and skin.	50	Hold my breath and turn away when someone coughs or sneezes. Exhale out mouth, then nose to blow germs away before inhaling.	Face the person and take three breaths in quick succession. Breathe as deeply as I can.	Don't blow air from my nose or mouth to "clear germs away" before breathing in.
Cashiering at work—I see a package of meat	Meat blood will get on me if I touch the package, even if it looks like the package is sealed.	50	Check other items first, leave it until last.	Because changing Lorraine's avoidant behavior would involve having her touch the package and touching is higher on her hierarchy, we let her keep this behavior until after her next exposure.	
Arriving at work—I look at the cash register	My coworkers don't wash their hands often enough. They're dirty from touching money and it's dangerous to touch anything they've touched.	65	Put cash drawer in with gloved hands. If no one's in line, spray register with cleaner and wipe with paper towels. If someone's in line, use only the tip of my index finger to touch the register buttons, then spray and wipe it as soon as possible.	1. Put cash drawer in without gloves on. 2. Touch register with both hands prior to putting gloves on to begin checking customers.	1. Put gloves on only after exposing myself to "dirty register." 2. Take only permitted number of breaks per shift. 3. On break, wash hands only after using the toilet. 4. Use toilet only if I genuinely need to. 5. Wash hands for no longer than thirty seconds with normal soap.

(continued on page 94)

TRIGGER SITUATION, THOUGHT OR IMAGE	AUTOMATIC THOUGHTS	SUD 1–100	COMPULSION/RITUAL/ NEUTRALIZING BEHAVIOR	EXPOSURE RULES	RESPONSE PREVENTION RULES
Touching a package of fish	Fish are icky, stinky, and full of germs, and now those germs are on my gloves. They'll multiply and get to my skin, and I'll get sick.	70–80	Put plastic bag over my left hand, grab item, and pull bag up and over it with my right hand. Wash hands on break.	Pick up package of fish with gloved hand. Put it in plastic bag; be sure to touch the package with both hands.	Same rules as above regarding hand washing on breaks.
Touching a package of chicken	Chicken blood is full of salmonella. It could kill me.	90	Put plastic bag over my left hand, grab item, and pull bag up and over it with my right hand. Ask for break if I get too anxious. Wash hands on break until I feel clean. Sometimes that takes ten minutes with hot water and a lot of soap.	Home practice: sister to bring package of chicken and beef over. Touch package of chicken with bare hands. Hold package tightly, then rub hands together, and rub them on my arms, body, legs, face, and hair. Touch package with a small cloth or paper towel, rub it with my hands, then all over my body and put in pocket for the rest of day. Sit and experience discomfort until it diminishes.	1. Wash hands only after discomfort has subsided to SUD less than 40. 2. Wash hands for no longer than thirty seconds with normal soap. 3. Do not shower until following morning. 4. After washing or showering, recontaminate myself by rubbing exposure cloth all over body again.
Touching a package of beef	Beef blood could have mad cow disease. It could kill me.	95	Put plastic bag over my left hand, grab item, and pull bag up and over it with my right hand. Ask for break if I get too anxious. Wash hands on break until I feel clean. Sometimes that takes ten minutes with hot water and a lot of soap.	Same procedure as with chicken package.	Same rules as above.

TRIGGER SITUATION, THOUGHT OR IMAGE	AUTOMATIC THOUGHTS	SUD 1–100	COMPULSION/RITUAL/ NEUTRALIZING BEHAVIOR	EXPOSURE RULES	RESPONSE PREVENTION RULES
Being near my nephew after work without showering first	I'm contaminated. He'll get it too and get sick and die.	100	Go home and shower before visiting. If I need to drop something off before showering, leave it on her porch, then call on cell phone after I'm in the car again.	Drive to sister's home directly from work, hug nephew, rub hands on his back, hold his hands, caress his face, and stroke his hair. Sit and experience the discomfort until it subsides.	1. Don't take shower before going to sister's. 2. Shower only in the morning for a maximum of fifteen minutes using normal soap. Set a kitchen timer in the bathroom to signal end of shower. Turn shower off immediately when timer rings. 3. Recontaminate myself by rubbing contamination cloth all over my body, face, and hair before dressing and then again after dressing. Carry contamination cloth in my pocket. 4. Recontaminate myself with contamination cloth after washing my hands throughout the day.

Almost certainly, your rules are different from the rules we devised for Lorraine. In fact, the rules she actually followed were slightly different than the rules as written. Some things were easier than anticipated and one was more difficult. Because her anxiety about touching money was not particularly high, she was able to do that exposure without too much difficulty once

she set her mind to it. She did this exposure two days in a row at home before she was able to follow the rule at work and touch the cash drawer without gloves. As it turned out, once she did that exposure several days in a row her new absence of fear of touching money made the subsequent task of touching the "dirty" cash register somewhat easier. She began by touching the sides of the register without gloves on her hands and after a break worked her way up to touching the keys of the register. Touching the keys was more problematic because she knew other cashiers had touched meat packages and then the register keys and had pushed the cash drawer closed with their "dirty hands." That exposure was quite uncomfortable for her, but by the time she was ready for it she was thoroughly versed in ERP and willing to endure the discomfort. Also, remember that Lorraine was simultaneously nearing the end of her exposures to the gas pumps when she began this exposure hierarchy. Therefore, she had a lot of trust and confidence in the process. Even with that experience, however, these exposures were work for her. The ingrained nature of OCD habits requires effort to undo.

Exposure to coughing and sneezing was more complicated than we initially considered. People in the supermarket line often cleared their throats or coughed a bit, but she went a couple of days with no sneezes at the register. Taking several quick breaths after someone cleared his/her throat was easy, but considerably more difficult after they coughed or hacked, and when someone finally sneezed she couldn't resist holding her breath. With patience and determination, however, she was able succeed in that exposure also. But there were some distinctions that Lorraine made that might be helpful for you to know about.

Part of her difficulty with this particular exposure was that people didn't sneeze very often and that made it difficult to practice. Second, she made a logical distinction between contamination—say, from touching money or even blood—versus exposure to a sneeze.

Intellectually, she knew that touching dirty objects would not cause her or her nephew to die. She knew that even if there were germs in those things, such as salmonella in chicken blood, they really wouldn't get into her digestive system unless she put them in her mouth or licked her fingers. She also knew that touching something dirty or germy would not really transfer to her nephew through a hug. (She didn't act as though she knew this, but intellectually she did.) However, she also knew that sneezes put real germs into the air and that an actual method of transmission was to breathe those germs.

To help Lorraine proceed with exposure to sneezes we needed to explore some thinking errors that clouded her ability to complete this item on her exposure hierarchy. Lorraine's fear of contamination from money or meat employed a thinking error called "magical thinking." (We discussed thinking errors in detail in chapter 5.) An example of magical thinking was her belief that touching something with her pants led to her entire body being contaminated. Her fear of exposure to cold germs represented a different type of thinking error, one called "catastrophic thinking." This means that Lorraine confused the real danger of catching a cold with the danger of dying or killing her nephew. Once she was clear that her exposure rule of three quick breaths after a sneeze represented a risk of a few days of congestion or runny nose (and not death), she was able to utilize the exposure to get over her unrealistic fear and compulsive avoidant behavior.

Initially, it seemed like a good idea that her exposure to packaged fish would occur in the store with gloved hands and that she would subsequently do it with her bare hands at home. When the time approached, she opted to do it all at home with bare hands rather than risk being overwhelmed by discomfort at work. Lorraine arranged for four days off to work on her exposure to packages of meat. She used the important principle of "massed exposure" during those four days. The first day she worked on the package of fish three separate times. Each repetition was substantially easier. The next day she started with the fish and then proceeded to the package of chicken, twice. The third and fourth days she exposed herself to the chicken and beef packages.

When touching closed packages of meat presented no difficulty, Lorraine made the bold decision to up the ante and touch raw meat and blood. This was an important step because she knew that on returning to work she would touch the occasional package that had leaked. She didn't want to backslide at work and revert to wearing gloves. Although the raw meat exposures were uncomfortable, they were also a triumph. Once she was able to do that, she knew she had conquered something she had previously imagined impossible.

Exposure Rules for Contaminants

Before going on to the next example, let's get clear on how to do a highly effective exposure to contaminants. The following method is tried and true. Using it will free you of your OCD in the least amount of time. Let's look more closely at Lorraine's exposure rule for meat packages and examine its components. *"Touch package of chicken with bare hands. Hold package tightly, then rub hands together, and rub them on my arms, body, legs, face,*

and hair. Touch package with a small cloth or paper towel, rub it with my hands, then all over my body and put in pocket for the rest of day. Sit and experience discomfort until it diminishes. Don't wash hands until after using bathroom and then only for fifteen to twenty seconds. Do not shower until following morning. After washing or showering, rub exposure cloth all over body again."

Lorraine's example contains the main elements of effective exposure. They worked for her and can work for you. Here are the essential ingredients of successful exposure.

1. Touch the trigger object firmly with both hands.
2. Rub your hands together.
3. Rub your hands on your arms, torso, legs, face, and hair.
4. Touch a small bit of cloth, handkerchief, or paper towel to the trigger object.
5. Rub the cloth with your hands and all over your body, including your face and hair.
6. Rub the contamination cloth on your pillow, bed sheets, chairs, the clothes in your closet, dishes, purse, wallet, doorknobs, steering wheel, etc. If you don't want something contaminated, that's exactly the thing you need to rub with your contamination cloth.
7. Put the cloth in your pocket and carry it with you throughout the day.
8. Avoid washing your hands for as long as possible.
9. Sit and observe your discomfort and the thoughts that get triggered.
10. Record your SUD score every ten minutes.

11. Continue the exposure until your SUD score is 30 or less, or until you need to go do something else.

12. If you wash your hands or shower, rub the contamination cloth all over your body again.

These are the rules for effective exposure with response prevention. You probably don't want to do this. That's normal. And that's the reason you start with triggers with low SUD scores. Start with a trigger that is not so disturbing. Do it, feel okay about doing it, get the hang of it. Then move on to the next item in your hierarchy. If you want to get your OCD under control ASAP, this is the way to succeed.

Rules for Washing and Bathing

Now let's talk about rules for normal washing and bathing. People with obsessive thoughts of contamination generally have highly ritualistic washing and bathing habits. The above ERP rules would be sufficient if it weren't for the fact that people often have trouble with the response prevention part. If you've been washing ritualistically for a long time, it will take some effort and willpower to retrain yourself back to normal washing. Let's define normal washing so you know what to compare your behavior to. (The following guidelines are adapted from treatment recommendations presented at a seminar sponsored by the OC Foundation, led by Dr. Alec Pollard of the Saint Louis Behavioral Medicine Institute.)

"Normal" Hand Washing

- Maximum fifteen times per day
- Thirty seconds maximum, about the amount of time it takes to sing "Happy Birthday" twice
- Use normal soap (no antimicrobial formulations, cleansers, or bleach solutions)
- When: before and after eating, after using the toilet, when hands are noticeably soiled, or when exposed to a trigger higher on the exposure hierarchy than you are currently working on
- Recontaminate yourself after washing; use trigger object or contamination cloth and follow exposure rules above

"Normal" Showering

- Once a day maximum
- Fifteen minutes maximum; set a kitchen timer or alarm, or ask your support person to time you
- Each body part soaped and rinsed only once
- When (to maximize exposure and minimize neutralizing your discomfort):
    - If you fear contaminating other people, shower only prior to going to bed
    - If you fear getting/being contaminated, shower only after getting up
- Recontaminate yourself after showering; use trigger object or contamination cloth and follow exposure rules above

Response Prevention Guidelines for Contaminants

The previous guidelines describe a "normal" degree of washing and showering. Your OCD may require more stringent cutbacks if you are not able to adhere to those guidelines. The more severe your OCD, the more beneficial it will be to restrict washing even further.

Edna Foa and Michael Kozak, two recognized experts on OCD, describe an intensive three-week treatment program that permits one ten-minute shower every three days and no hand washing whatsoever. The more stringently you regulate your washing, the less tempted you will be to ritualize "accidentally." Specify in your ERP rules how many times you may hand wash and under what conditions. Make your ERP rules as though you were writing a contract with yourself. Try to anticipate how and when you might try to wriggle out of the contract. If you find you can't adhere to your response prevention rules, you may need to make them stricter (i.e., wash less), rather than making them looser, as you may be tempted to do.

ERP Lite

If you aren't ready to jump in and begin full-bore ERP, the following may be a less intimidating way to start. Remember that ORDER-ABC is an acronym for:

- Observe your thoughts
- Remind yourself that your obsessions are OCD
- Do something different, delay your compulsive behavior
- Expose yourself to your trigger situations, thoughts, or images
- Response prevention: stop yourself from doing any neutralizing rituals
- Allow your Brain to Change

It's possible to begin loosening OCD's hold on you by gradually altering or delaying your rituals. This won't be as quick or as dramatic in producing results as ERP with massed practice, but it can slowly lessen OCD's severity. This technique requires you to be more of an observer of your thoughts and behaviors and to conduct some experiments. Try to watch your stream of thoughts and images as though you were sitting in a theater. Identify yourself with the one who is watching the thoughts. Say to yourself, "I'm not going to get caught up in my thoughts. I'm just going to watch how one leads to the next." As the thoughts get more intense, again comment on what's happening: "OCD is working hard to hook me. I feel my body getting

(continued on page 100)

more uncomfortable." Developing the capacity to watch your fearful thoughts instead of simply believing them and acting on them is the core of "mindfulness." Mindfulness has been getting a lot of research attention in recent years. It has been shown to help reduce anxiety and chronic pain levels and increase the immune response, and even help people with terminal cancer experience an improved quality of life.

Mindfulness involves watching your thoughts for as long as possible without getting wrapped up in believing them or acting on them. Sometimes people journal their thoughts to get more familiar with how thoughts can start with a simple concern and get blown out of proportion. Believing fearful or disturbing thoughts without questioning their accuracy activates the frontal lobes that immerse us in the experience. Watching the chain of thoughts and the process of becoming more and more fearful, on the other hand, helps develop the frontal lobes' executive function that can help lift you out of your discomfort and suffering.

Remind yourself that the thoughts you're watching are generated by OCD. Use this awareness to learn more about your OCD and in the process take some of its power away. Say to yourself something like, "This is OCD," or "OCD is really cruel," or a favorite from a noted expert on OCD, Dr. Jeffrey Schwartz, "It's not me, it's my OCD."

Watch your obsessive thoughts, and at the same time, do something different to delay your compulsive behavior. By delaying even for a short while, you're engaging in a modified form of exposure and response prevention. When you feel you can no longer delay your compulsive behavior, do it differently than you usually do. Watch your thoughts as you do it differently. It may help to utilize one of the relaxation techniques described in chapter 10 (see page 141). Again, observe yourself.

As you tolerate the discomfort and pay attention to the process, your brain is busy processing this new experience. These are the steps you need to do to allow your brain to change. Try to be consistent in *not* doing what you generally do automatically: obsess and compulsively neutralize. Instead, the next time your obsessive thoughts begin to bother you, try practicing the ORDER-ABC.

Thought Rituals

Let's have a look at how to get control over thought rituals. This is a bit different from other types of OCD in that the obsession and the ritual are both done in the mind. We say "a bit different," inasmuch as people with OCD try to mentally neutralize their discomfort. But in most forms of OCD there is also an overt behavior that can be observed and halted. (Some clinicians disagree with this and discuss what they call "pure obsessives," meaning people who only obsess and don't try to neutralize. Whether there are truly pure obsessives or just people with mental rituals that are hard to define, however, is an area needing research.)

When obsessions and the rituals that neutralize them are both mental, there are two major methods available to overcome this form of OCD. The first is a technique used in cognitive therapy to help you realize what your fear is and what negative "core belief" is beneath that fear. This is what we worked on in chapter 5.

Everyone has negative core beliefs that get triggered when we feel bad. Negative core beliefs for the most part are useless, except to keep us feeling bad and upset with ourselves. The more strenuously you hold on to these negative beliefs, the more difficult it is to combat them. While working to prevent rituals is important for everyone with OCD, it's especially important if your rituals are exclusively mental. If that's

the case for you, review chapter 5 and pay additional attention to those exercises.

Review the following list of common negative core beliefs (which we considered earlier in chapter 5) and put a checkmark next to the one or two that sound most familiar to you. Now write a statement about yourself next to the items that argue against it. Think of a specific time when you demonstrated a strength that proves the negative belief is wrong. For example, "I am very competent. Just recently I got up in the middle of the night when my sick child was having nightmares. I held her, talked with her, got her a cool drink, and rubbed her back until she fell asleep. She slept through the night and felt much better in the morning."

- I'm unlovable.
- I'm incompetent.
- I'm helpless.
- I'm undeserving.
- I'm powerless.
- I'm vulnerable.
- I'm bad/evil/wicked.
- I'm out of control/I'm crazy.
- I'm defective.
- I'm a failure.
- I'm weak.
- I'm needy.

As you might imagine, none of these beliefs does you any good. They only make you feel bad about yourself and make it harder to deal effectively with the world. Fortunately, these are only *beliefs* that we formed about ourselves when we were young children and genuinely dependent on others to care for us. When we are very young, all of us are needy, weak, vulnerable, powerless, etc. And you may have had parents who told you that you were unlovable, bad, defective, undeserving, a failure, or crazy. But none of that means it's true today. Even if you feel weaker or needier than other people around you, it doesn't mean that these traits define you. Everyone has moments of strength, resolve, cleverness, lovability, competence, and so on. The ability to remind yourself of those strengths, while you're feeling deficient, will make a difference in your campaign to conquer your OCD.

If you feel justified in holding one or more of the above beliefs and are not able to effectively argue against them, we recommend that you begin working with a psychotherapist. This is especially important before continuing on with the next method for working with mental rituals: imaginal exposure.

Imaginal exposure is a way of working with thought rituals that prevents them from neutralizing our anxiety. This is accomplished by writing, then reading, a script (or listening to a recorded version of it) that exposes you to your triggers and maintains the exposure for a prolonged period of time (just as we do with other forms of ERP). The script usually describes the most feared outcome and may even exaggerate the fear. Although it can be very anxiety provoking to

write and listen to, a script like this is a very effective way of quickly helping you realize how unrealistic your fears are.

This method can also be used when real-world exposures are difficult, expensive, or too threatening. Sometimes people will sit and imagine the real-world exposure they are planning to do. Once they feel more comfortable with it in their imagination, they feel more confident about accomplishing it in real life. It will be easier to understand this by working through an example.

Harm Obsessions—A Case of Postpartum OCD

One way thought rituals can manifest themselves is in a fear of harming one's loved ones, either intentionally or unintentionally. Although high levels of anxiety can occur with any type of OCD, harm obsessions are generally terrifying. One of the clearest examples of this is when OCD is triggered after the birth of a child. Although this can occur in fathers as well as mothers, it is probably more common in new mothers after the incredible hormonal storms that take place during pregnancy and childbirth. There is not yet a category called postpartum OCD, though this is an increasingly recognized time of onset.

Let's work through Lakeesha's example. Lakeesha, a twenty-eight-year-old female postal clerk with a six-month-old baby girl and eight-year-old daughter, lived with her mother. She came to treatment at her mother's insistence after persistent trouble getting out of bed to take care of little Jasmina. During Lakeesha's three-month maternity leave, her mother reported extreme difficulty in getting her to care for her baby. At first her mother thought it was fatigue, then she began to suspect depression. When Lakeesha returned to work from maternity leave, she often got up early and left for work, leaving her mother to take charge of both children.

Lakeesha was initially reluctant to talk about how she was feeling, and depression seemed obvious. As we began to work together on the depression, it became clear that there was more to it than that. Lakeesha first hinted at scary thoughts, then "thoughts too horrible to live with." With encouragement she finally opened up. Between sobs she began to describe some of the thoughts that plagued her daily. Her depression became readily understandable once she revealed her persistent thoughts that she would stab, smother, smash, drive over, or otherwise murder her infant. The vivid quality of these intrusive thoughts and images was so appalling to her that she didn't want to get out of bed or get close to Jasmina for fear that she would be overtaken by an irrepressible urge to kill her baby. When she returned to work, she felt like the baby was safe as long as she was out of the house. The thoughts were less intense at work, where she needed to focus on the tasks in front of her, though the images intruded there as well.

With much coaxing and coaching, Lakeesha was able to put words to the horrific images in her mind and the fear that she would actually follow through on her thoughts. She was modestly comforted when we explained the distinction between someone who fears killing her child and someone who might actually do it (discussed in greater detail later in this section). In fact, someone with OCD is the least likely person on the planet to harm her/his own child. Filling in the following chart was extremely difficult for Lakeesha. Making distinctions as to which images were the least fear provoking was in itself a form of exposure therapy, as she held an image in her mind and tried to compare that level of fear with the level invoked by other images. Lakeesha's driving force was the desire to be the good, loving mother she remembered herself to be with her first child, and she desperately wanted to be with Jasmina. Keeping that goal in mind helped Lakeesha succeed in treatment.

A key part of Lakeesha's treatment began well before she started ERP. Lakeesha needed to understand that she was regularly engaged in thinking errors. And she needed to see how this made it difficult for her to assess the actual chance of her harming Jasmina. As you review her automatic thoughts that resulted from exposure to her triggers, you'll notice that most of them involved believing that she might actually harm her baby. This is an example of the thinking error called "thought-action fusion." Recall from chapter 5 that this means that because she had a thought about harm she believed she was the type of person who might actually do it. Certainly, a mother who *wanted* to harm her child would be a bad or perhaps evil mother. Lakeesha, by contrast, lived in terror that she *might* do it. These, of course, are very different situations.

This belief that she was capable of going "out of control" or "going completely crazy" was a central theme of her fears and was based on her core belief that she was a defective person. There was no actual evidence from her life to support this core belief, though it took considerable work before Lakeesha was able to see that. Once she was able to even momentarily consider the possibility that she really was a good and loving mother, her anxiety lessened somewhat.

She also believed that her thoughts of harm had the potential to cause harm all by themselves. This is an example of "magical thinking," because a thought does not cause anything to happen in the world unless we act on it. After gaining some experience challenging the faulty basis of her fears, she was more ready to take on the work of ERP.

LAKEESHA'S ERP TREATMENT HIERARCHY CHART

Review Lakeesha's ERP Treatment Hierarchy Chart and think about how you would arrange exposure with response prevention to help her. Try to distinguish between neutralizing rituals that are mental versus behavioral. One of her behaviors, a very common one in OCD, is avoidance of trigger situations. Design a treatment plan that prevents her from avoiding triggers and engaging in mental rituals. Her ERP plan can use direct exposure as well as imaginal exposures. Read each line of her ERP Treatment Hierarchy Chart, then write your exposure with response prevention rules on the lines below it that correspond to each letter in the chart. What you do here for Lakeesha you will soon be able to do for yourself.

LAKEESHA'S ERP TREATMENT HIERARCHY CHART

TRIGGER SITUATION, THOUGHT, OR IMAGE	AUTOMATIC THOUGHTS	SUD 1–100	COMPULSION/RITUAL/NEUTRALIZING BEHAVIOR	EXPOSURE RULES	RESPONSE PREVENTION RULES
Getting ready to leave work	I worry that I might go home and do something terrible. Worry that there's something really wrong with me, that I must be crazy.	50–70	Ask for overtime. Sit in my car and pray for strength to do the right thing and to make me whole again. Read my Bible for at least an hour before going home.	A	A
Hearing Jasmina cry when she's in another room	I worry that something is terribly wrong with her and my thoughts about her dying will cause her to die.	60–70	Wait for my mother to go to her. Tell LaTonya to take care of her sister. Pray to the Lord.	B	B
Seeing Jasmina lying in her crib	I take a pillow and smother her. Then I break down on the floor and want to kill myself.	70–80	Leave the room quickly. Leave the house.	C	C
Hearing her cry when holding her	I worry I might accidentally hold her too tight or push her to my breast and smother her.	75	Ask my mother if I'm holding her too tight. Try to get my mother to take her. Give her a bottle so I know where her face and nose are.	D	D
Holding Jasmina	I'm afraid I'll drop her or throw her against the floor. Her head splits open and she dies.	75–90	Sit down on the floor with her, put pillows around. Have mother or LaTonya with me. Pray.	E	E
Feeding Jasmina	I jam food into her mouth and cram it in until she chokes. I see a panicked look in her eyes and do nothing to save her.	100	Pray the Lord strikes me dead if I start to do anything that might harm my baby. Stay at work or in bed so mother feeds her. Ask LaTonya to watch me and tell me if I do anything wrong.	F	F

A. Exposure Rules:

B. Exposure Rules:

C. Exposure Rules:

D. Exposure Rules:

E. Exposure Rules:

F. Exposure Rules:

A. Response Prevention Rules:

B. Response Prevention Rules:

C. Response Prevention Rules::

D. Response Prevention Rules:

E. Response Prevention Rules:

F. Response Prevention Rules:

Compare the exposure with response prevention rules that you thought of with the ones in Lakeesha's treatment plan. Don't worry if you came up with different ideas of what she should do. The most important thing is that you really think through the example and make it a meaningful exercise. This is the best way to prepare to make your own treatment plan.

LAKEESHA'S ERP TREATMENT HIERARCHY CHART

TRIGGER SITUATION, THOUGHT, OR IMAGE	AUTOMATIC THOUGHTS	SUD 1–100	COMPULSION/RITUAL/ NEUTRALIZING BEHAVIOR	EXPOSURE RULES	RESPONSE PREVENTION RULES
Getting ready to leave work	I worry I might go home and do something terrible. Worry that there's something really wrong with me, that I must be crazy.	50–70	Ask for overtime. Sit in my car and pray for strength to do the right thing and to make me whole again. Read my Bible for at least an hour before going home.	Sit in my car after work and listen to my digital recorder for an hour. Note: digital recorder contains imaginal exposure script that follows chart.	1. Don't ask for overtime during the duration of my treatment. Say "no" if it's offered, unless mandatory. 2. I won't read the Bible while in the car.
Hearing Jasmina cry when she's in another room	I worry that something is terribly wrong with her and my thoughts about her dying will cause her to die.	60–70	Wait for my mother to go to her. Tell LaTonya to take care of her sister. Pray to the Lord.	Go to Jasmina, hold her while I'm sitting on the floor. Pick her up after Mother or LaTonya get to the room also.	1. Make agreements with Mother and LaTonya that they are not to care for Jasmina when I'm home. 2. One of them will supervise me when I'm holding Jasmina but they will not respond to my questions asking for reassurance. 3. I will stop whatever I'm doing and go to her within fifteen seconds of hearing her cry. 4. I will not pray while holding Jasmina. I will talk to her the entire time.
Seeing Jasmina lying in her crib	I take a pillow and smother her. Then I break down on the floor and want to kill myself.	70–80	Leave the room quickly. Leave the house.	1. Sit in the chair across from the crib. 2. Allow my thoughts to happen. Watch them until they diminish.	1. I'm not allowed to escape the situation. 2. I will not pray during this time. 3. Do this with Mother or LaTonya silently in the room with me. 4. When ready, sit in room without Mother or LaTonya.

(continued on page 108)

TRIGGER SITUATION, THOUGHT, OR IMAGE	AUTOMATIC THOUGHTS	SUD 1–100	COMPULSION/RITUAL/ NEUTRALIZING BEHAVIOR	EXPOSURE RULES	RESPONSE PREVENTION RULES
Hearing her cry when holding her	I worry I might accidentally hold her too tight or push her to my breast and smother her.	75	Ask my mother if I'm holding her too tight. Try to get my mother to take her. Give her a bottle so I know where her face and nose are.	1. Hold Jasmina while sitting on the floor without Mother or LaTonya in the room.	1. Mother and LaTonya are to leave the room and not take over even if I ask. 2. Allow my thoughts; watch them without praying.
Holding Jasmina	I'm afraid I'll drop her or throw her against the floor. Her head splits open and she dies.	75–90	Sit down on the floor with her, put pillows around. Have mother or LaTonya with me. Pray.	Hold Jasmina while standing without Mother or LaTonya in the room.	1. Mother and LaTonya are to leave the room and not take over even if I ask.
Feeding Jasmina	I jam food into her mouth and cram it in until she chokes. I see a panicked look in her eyes and do nothing to save her.	100	Pray the Lord strikes me dead if I start to do anything that might harm my baby. Stay at work or in bed so mother feeds her. Ask LaTonya to watch me and tell me if I do anything wrong.	Feed Jasmina when I'm home.	1. Talk to Jasmina so I can't pray while feeding her. 2. Don't pray aloud. 3. Mother or LaTonya in the room, but silent, no reassurance. 4. When I'm ready, no one else in the room while I feed Jasmina.

We hope you took the time to think of your own way to treat Lakeesha before comparing it with our ERP treatment plan for her. And hopefully, you see the logic of how her plan was constructed. It systematically tackled each trigger while allowing her to continue her avoidance and neutralizing behaviors for items with higher SUDs.

To start with, she wrote and recorded (on a digital recorder) several scripts like the one that follows. She spent many days listening to her scripts over and over again until they only evoked a slight degree of nervousness. This experience, which was enormously difficult at first, began to help her see that she was not the kind of person who could hurt her child. The more she listened to her scripts, the more she began to think they were ridiculous. Yet at the same time she continued to have intrusive images that made her doubt herself and continue to avoid contact with Jasmina. Once she gained a degree of confidence through imaginal exposure, she began the hierarchy of actual exposure situations described in her treatment chart.

The following script goes directly to the heart of Lakeesha's fears. That's what makes the script work. You might find it objectionable. Indeed, if this were what she really wanted to do, it would be quite horrific. However, as we discussed earlier, people with OCD are generally terrified that they might hurt someone. This is quite the opposite of someone who actually wants to cause harm. People with postpartum OCD, quite understandably, spend enormous mental and emotional energy trying to avoid the kinds of images described below. The reason for that goes back to false core beliefs about oneself, such as being evil, defective, or incapable of love.

Lakeesha's Imaginal Exposure Script

I look at the clock and see it's time to go home from work. I told Mother I'd go straight home today. I hesitate before starting the car. I look at the Bible in the seat next to me. I think, "If I don't pray about this first something bad will happen." But I don't stop to pray or read the Bible. I start the car and drive. I know I should pray but I don't. I'm driving home feeling more and more nervous, the closer I get to home. I park the car and my hands are sweaty, I feel nervous and shaky. I tell myself I'll be okay but as I walk in the door, I hear Jasmina crying. I see Mother napping on the sofa. I walk past the bedroom and ignore Jasmina. I go to the kitchen. I think, "This is my chance—no one will stop me." I get a knife from the kitchen and go to Jasmina's crib. She is crying and sees me coming. I lean over the crib and she stops crying, looking at me, expecting me to pick her up

and comfort her. Instead, I raise the knife up and bring it down into her soft little stomach, as her eyes bulge in disbelief that her mother could do such a thing. I don't care, I feel glad that I did it. I stand there watching her bleed. I'm happy she's dying. I decide to stab her again because it feels good. Mother runs in and see me standing with the bloody knife raised in the air. She pushes me away and scoops Jasmina up in her arms. Mother looks at me. She looks shocked and can't believe what I've done. She tries to stop the bleeding but can't. Mother's hands are full of blood, while Jasmina's body goes into convulsions. Mother rushes to the phone and calls 911. I sit down in the chair near the crib. I'm happy. I start laughing. I feel great. I always knew I was a killer and now I am one and I love it. Then I realize what I've done. Suddenly I'm horrified. I go toward Jasmina to try to save her but Mother knocks me down. I yell, "We have to save her." Mother screams at me, "You killed her. You're crazy—I knew it—you're crazy. You're evil. Get away from her." She looks at me with hatred and disgust.

I hear the sirens of emergency vehicles stopping in front of the house. The emergency people rush in. The first one in takes Jasmina and puts her on the floor. He tries to resuscitate her but can't. He looks over and sees me with the bloody knife still in my hand and yells, "Arrest her." The other rescue people grab me and push me from the room to two policemen who just arrived. The police look in at the floor and see Jasmina and then look at me very angrily. One of them says, "I can't believe my eyes. You did this? You sick bitch, you're going where you'll never see daylight again." They hold me and handcuff me and force me to look back at Jasmina. The cop says, "Look at that, you pervert. Let that image burn in your mind and terrorize you every minute of the rest of your God-forsaken life. And when you die you'll rot in hell and burn for eternity."

As mentioned above, this script is pretty graphic and probably uncomfortable to read. However, this is what makes the script effective. Our thoughts can be very cruel to us. When we're investing a lot of energy resisting and neutralizing them, we can't examine and reflect on them. Listening to a script over and over again results in habituation and decreased emotional reactivity. This permits your objective, rational mind to see how ridiculous your fear is and respond to the needs of the moment. Repeated exposure leads to increasingly accurate interpretation such as, "These images are just my OCD. I would never do something like that. I'm a competent, loving mother who knows how to care for my baby. Let me focus on what she needs instead of being distracted by irrelevant thoughts."

Here is a list of key elements that make imaginal exposure scripts effective:

- **Write in the first person, present tense: "I walk," "I pick up the knife," "I stab her."**
- **Describe the scene as vividly as you can.**
- **Describe your worst fears as though they are actually taking place.**
- **If needed, write a series of increasingly frightening scripts.**
- **Get to the point where your scripts are more exaggerated than your fears.**

Listen to them over and over again at each sitting until you notice some reduction in your anxiety—this might take thirty to ninety minutes or longer.

Observe your thoughts and emotional reactions as you listen. The more you focus on what you're doing, the sooner your anxiety will diminish.

Expose yourself to the script one or more times a day until it doesn't provoke discomfort greater than 40 SUDs.

Write a new, even more disturbing script or move on to actual exposure situations.

Perfection and Order

Let's look at an ERP Treatment Hierarchy Chart for Paul, an architect who was compulsive about keeping his office, desk, and home belongings perfectly arranged. When possessions got out of perfect alignment or messed up by mean-spirited coworkers, Paul got very uncomfortable. He didn't obsess about bad things happening or catastrophic consequences, as some people with this form of OCD might. Paul simply got upset until he put things "back to rights." In constructing his treatment plan, Paul made decisions about how much "mess" he was willing to tolerate and how quickly. He wanted to go slowly and have modest exposures at work and home simultaneously.

Rather than have you work through the example, we'll show you some of the main elements of his treatment chart. We hope, by now, you've got the hang of creating exposure with response prevention rules and would be able to do this example rather handily, even if your plan looks different than the one below.

PAUL'S ERP TREATMENT HIERARCHY CHART

TRIGGER SITUATION, THOUGHT, OR IMAGE	AUTOMATIC THOUGHTS	SUD 1–100	COMPULSION/RITUAL/ NEUTRALIZING BEHAVIOR	EXPOSURE RULES	RESPONSE PREVENTION RULES
Enter office cubicle in the morning, cleaning person left the wastebasket out of square with the desk	Oh, God, I hate it when they do that. I've left notes for them, but they never get it right. I can't do anything until everything is set to rights.	45	Straighten wastebasket immediately.	1. Leave wastebasket wherever it was put by cleaning person. 2. Sit and look at it for as long as work duties allow.	Don't touch or move it for the entire week.
Arrive home, hang jacket in closet	My jacket needs to be next to the overcoat but not touching it. All hangers should be two inches apart.	50	Hang jacket in same place as always, properly spaced.	Put jacket on hanger and hang without looking. Run hand roughly across all hangers to "muss" their arrangement. Sit in front of closet and examine the result.	Don't touch or rearrange hangers. Pay attention to them until SUD score is 40 or less. Close closet door without rearranging anything.

(continued on page 112)

TRIGGER SITUATION, THOUGHT, OR IMAGE	AUTOMATIC THOUGHTS	SUD 1–100	COMPULSION/RITUAL/ NEUTRALIZING BEHAVIOR	EXPOSURE RULES	RESPONSE PREVENTION RULES
I finish a task at the computer. The computer mouse must be positioned at top right of the mouse pad.	It just doesn't feel right until it is in its proper place. I must put it there.	55	Put mouse where it belongs when using the phone or stepping away from my desk.	Leave mouse on the desk, off mouse pad. Push it away with enough force to move it several inches. Leave it where it stops. Sit and notice how I feel.	1. Leave mouse there for full ten minutes one time in a.m. and once during afternoon. 2. Same at lunchtime for at least ten minutes. If possible, leave cubicle and go to lunch. 3. Same at end of workday. Leave and go home without straightening, if possible. 4. Continue daily until able to leave it.
Someone visiting my apartment, especially sitting on the sofa and moving the pillows.	That's not how it's supposed to be. I can hardly stand it.	70	Avoid inviting people to my apartment or sit with them at dining table. Rearrange anything they move as quickly as possible.	Invite sister over with agreed-on plan to change things around room by room. Sit in silence while SUD level declines. Then go to the next room and repeat.	Leave rearranged items where she put them for at least a week. Sit and view them several times/day. If I use something, put it somewhere other than where it's "supposed to go."
Sight of unmade bed in the morning	I must make the bed perfectly. I can't leave the bedroom until it's done.	75	Make the bed right after dressing. Sheet, blanket, and bed-spread must be perfectly flat.	Leave the bed unmade. Go have breakfast. Observe my thoughts and discomfort during breakfast.	After breakfast return to bedroom and walk in and out until discomfort is under 40 or half hour of exposure. Leave the house without making the bed.

As with the previous examples, Paul's ERP therapy enabled him to tackle the problems with the lowest SUD ratings before the more difficult exposures. By gaining confidence with easier items he was able to move through the hierarchy. Not all exposures proceeded smoothly. Some were more difficult than anticipated and needed to be repeated and modified over the course of several weeks. For example, initially Paul felt his sister moved things "too much" and he put things back after she left. Fortunately, she was able to return and continue to disturb his exact placement of objects in his home. Eventually, she rearranged some of his furniture and on a subsequent visit rearranged it further so that it was not only in "the wrong place" but was also out of square with the walls or other pieces of furniture. Finally, Paul was able to be the one to misarrange things in his apartment (e.g., drawers half open with underwear hanging partially out) and leave them like that for days at a time without being overly bothered.

There is certainly an element of trial and error in designing and implementing a successful treatment plan. If something doesn't work, it simply means you need to understand what went wrong and modify your plan so it does work. Generally problems arise from trying to take on an exposure you weren't yet ready for or telling yourself it's okay to do your ritual "just this once, because . . ." Don't give up! And don't give in! If you have a setback, it doesn't mean that this method doesn't work for you. It simply means you need to modify your plan. Your OCD is going to try to tell you that you can't do it. Don't listen. You can succeed!

In this chapter, you considered several case studies of common forms of OCD. We challenged you to write treatment plans for those people to help you begin thinking like a cognitive-behavioral therapist. By working through the examples, you have gained practical insight into how exposure is conducted in a way that works and how to structure response prevention rules to make maximum use of the exposure. As a result of this experience, you should have a much better sense of how to approach your own situation.

It is likely that the trigger chart you completed in chapter 6 is not as thorough as the ones in the examples. In the next chapter, you'll have a chance to review and update your trigger information as you begin constructing an ERP Treatment Hierarchy Chart for yourself.

Chapter 9

My ORDER-ABC Treatment Plan

Now it's time to put everything you've learned to use and develop your own individualized treatment plan. For maximum results, begin with the obsession that causes you the most difficulty. By getting that under control, you will get the most symptom relief in the shortest time. This may or may not be the same topic you practiced with earlier in the book when you filled in your Obsessive Thoughts Trigger Chart. If that's what you want to work on, great, you've got some preliminary work already done. If, after reading the intervening chapters, you've decided to work on something different, that's fine, too.

The first chart in this chapter is slightly different from what you've been working with thus far. It combines the various elements you've learned about and gives you enough room to write. Begin by filling in the trigger situations, automatic thoughts, and SUD ratings. You might want to jot down some thoughts on a blank sheet of paper prior to transferring them to the chart. That will give you a chance to rearrange them in order of their SUD ratings.

The first trigger item you transfer to your treatment chart should rate at least 40 to 45 SUDs. Then write the automatic thoughts that occur in response to that trigger. Next, identify which type of thinking error your automatic thought represents. You may need to review chapter 5 and the thinking error types you identified as the ones you most frequently engage in. Document your thinking errors for each automatic thought. Knowing that you are engaging in thinking errors will help you during your ERP. Knowing the specific type of thinking error your thoughts represent will give you greater ability to tolerate the discomfort of ERP.

Treatment Plan Checklist

1. Decide whether you want to include medication as part of your treatment. If you do, make an appointment with a psychiatrist and get started, if you haven't already done so.

2. Fill out a detailed ERP Treatment Hierarchy Chart for the obsession that most bothers you.

3. Talk with family, friends, and coworkers you want to help you succeed in your treatment.

4. Make up a Support Agreement form (see pages 131–132) with each person who will help you during treatment. Specify what kind of help you would like from them, as well as what they will refrain from doing.

5. Schedule time to engage in ERP treatment. Fill in the treatment calendar so you're clear on your plan, and stick to it.

6. Arrange/schedule with others if you want their presence and encouragement.

7. If you're going to use imaginal exposure, write your first script and read it into your recorder.

8. Begin ERP with the lowest SUD trigger identified in your treatment plan.

9. Expose yourself to the trigger and stay with it. Let your brain do the work of rewiring itself.

10. Work through your exposure hierarchy one item at a time.

11. Conquer each trigger before moving on to the next one.

12. Do something nice to reward yourself after your exposure sessions. This is hard work. Consider doing something relaxing afterward, such as going out for a meal, a movie, or a nature walk, playing with your child or pet, reading something fun, or even just taking a nap.

Now you're ready for the most challenging part of developing your ERP treatment plan. Write down exactly how you intend to expose yourself to the trigger and exactly what you will do and not do as part of your response prevention plan. Once you've done that for the first trigger, move on to the one with the next higher SUD rating.

Once you've completed this for all the triggers, review your treatment plan with your support person. This review is very important for several reasons. One reason is thoroughness. It's very difficult to think through your own situation objec-

tively. Having someone else ask, "What are you going to do if ..." helps you think through possible difficulties before they occur. In that way, you're better prepared to succeed. The second very important reason to review this with someone else is that thinking and talking about each trigger, exposure plan, and response prevention rule is a form of imaginal exposure. This additional exposure helps begin the process of rewiring your brain circuits and will help you get through it more easily. Third, it's very helpful to "be on the same page" with the person who will be cheering you on.

TRIGGER SITUATION, THOUGHT, OR IMAGE	AUTOMATIC THOUGHTS	THINKING ERROR	SUD 1–100	COMPULSION/RITUAL/ NEUTRALIZING BEHAVIOR

Exposure Rules:

Response Prevention Rules:

TRIGGER SITUATION, THOUGHT, OR IMAGE	AUTOMATIC THOUGHTS	THINKING ERROR	SUD 1–100	COMPULSION/RITUAL/ NEUTRALIZING BEHAVIOR

Exposure Rules:

Response Prevention Rules:

TRIGGER SITUATION, THOUGHT, OR IMAGE	AUTOMATIC THOUGHTS	THINKING ERROR	SUD 1–100	COMPULSION/RITUAL/ NEUTRALIZING BEHAVIOR

Exposure Rules:

Response Prevention Rules:

TRIGGER SITUATION, THOUGHT, OR IMAGE	AUTOMATIC THOUGHTS	THINKING ERROR	SUD 1–100	COMPULSION/RITUAL/ NEUTRALIZING BEHAVIOR

Exposure Rules:

Response Prevention Rules:

TRIGGER SITUATION, THOUGHT, OR IMAGE	AUTOMATIC THOUGHTS	THINKING ERROR	SUD 1–100	COMPULSION/RITUAL/ NEUTRALIZING BEHAVIOR

Exposure Rules:

Response Prevention Rules:

TRIGGER SITUATION, THOUGHT, OR IMAGE	AUTOMATIC THOUGHTS	THINKING ERROR	SUD 1–100	COMPULSION/RITUAL/ NEUTRALIZING BEHAVIOR

Exposure Rules:

Response Prevention Rules:

TRIGGER SITUATION, THOUGHT, OR IMAGE	AUTOMATIC THOUGHTS	THINKING ERROR	SUD 1–100	COMPULSION/RITUAL/ NEUTRALIZING BEHAVIOR

Exposure Rules:

Response Prevention Rules:

TRIGGER SITUATION, THOUGHT, OR IMAGE	AUTOMATIC THOUGHTS	THINKING ERROR	SUD 1–100	COMPULSION/RITUAL/ NEUTRALIZING BEHAVIOR

Exposure Rules:

_____

_____

Response Prevention Rules:

_____

_____

TRIGGER SITUATION, THOUGHT, OR IMAGE	AUTOMATIC THOUGHTS	THINKING ERROR	SUD 1–100	COMPULSION/RITUAL/ NEUTRALIZING BEHAVIOR

Exposure Rules:

_____

_____

Response Prevention Rules:

_____

_____

TRIGGER SITUATION, THOUGHT, OR IMAGE	AUTOMATIC THOUGHTS	THINKING ERROR	SUD 1–100	COMPULSION/RITUAL/ NEUTRALIZING BEHAVIOR

Exposure Rules:

- -

- -

Response Prevention Rules:

- -

- -

Now that you have your ERP treatment plan and have reviewed it with your support person(s), there's a little more planning to do before launching into treatment.

My Treatment Schedule

Probably the most common anxiety reduction strategy is to avoid triggers. You surely have noticed your own reluctance to engage in certain activities, go specific places, or talk about a certain topic in order to avoid triggering your obsession. So it should be no surprise to learn that people who begin an OCD self-help program frequently think of excuses to avoid treatment.

However, we have some good news for you. The fact that you've gotten this far in the book is proof that you have at least two very powerful things working in your favor. One is that you understand now what you need to do in order to get better, and are committed to doing it. The second is that by having done the exercises up to this point, you have already begun treatment. You've given thought to what your triggers are and quantified with a SUD score how much anxiety they induce. You've given thought to how you would expose yourself to those triggers and what response prevention rules you could employ. You might also have given some thought to, or even written, an imaginal exposure script. And you probably also have a better understanding than the average person as to how your negative automatic thoughts and negative core beliefs have interfered with your ability to combat uncomfortable thoughts. So the fact that you've already begun treatment is a huge advantage in taking it a step further. For you, starting ERP with a trigger of about 40 to 45 SUDs should be a relatively small step forward—with a big payback.

The systematic plan you've developed here will make you more successful in carrying out your treatment than people utilizing less structured approaches. The detailed nature of your ERP plan will make it easier for you to gain experience and confidence step by step. By never overwhelming yourself, you'll work through your exposure hierarchy with increasing belief in your ability to successfully rewire your OCD.

To minimize the problem of avoidance and maximize your treatment gains, it is important to create a schedule and stick to it as best you can. As we've said, the more frequently and more intensively you practice ERP, the sooner you will tame your disorder. By making the necessary arrangements to free your time of other obligations you will increase your likelihood of success.

ERP: How Often and How Long?

It is impossible to predict how long it will take you to get the kind of results you desire. Most estimates of treatment duration are for therapist-assisted programs working with moderate to severe cases of OCD. Factors such as the type of OCD you have, and the severity of your symptoms, will have a lot to do with how long your treatment will need to be. Successful treatment is minimally defined as significant symptom relief, obsessive thoughts and ritual behaviors reduced by at least 50 percent, and noticeably improved daily functioning. Although dramatic improvement can be anticipated during the active treatment phase, many people note ongoing improvements during the next six to twelve months as they continue to employ ERP principles during routine activities (we'll discuss this in chapter 13, "Prevent Relapse with ORDER-ABC").

The following chart is a "ballpark" guideline intended to help you get a feel for what you will need to do to get the kind of results you want. These estimates assume that your OCD is moderately severe, that each ERP session lasts at least 90 to 120 minutes, and that there are two or more ERP sessions per treatment day. Less severe symptoms require less intense treatment.

ERP TREATMENT DURATION GUIDELINES

TIME TO IMPROVEMENT	TREATMENT DAYS/WEEK
2–3 weeks	5–7
3–4 weeks	4
4–5 weeks	3
5+ weeks	2

Think realistically about what is going on in your life and the practicalities of how you will accomplish your program. Then answer the following questions and compare your answers with the chart above. Are your treatment goals consistent with your ability to commit time to your treatment?

- **I plan to significantly reduce my OCD symptoms in: (circle one) 2–3 weeks, 3–4 weeks, 4–5 weeks, 5+ weeks**
- **I intend to pursue my treatment: (circle one) aggressively moderately casually**
- **I intend to engage in OCD self-treatment _____ days a week.**
- **On treatment days, I intend to engage in ERP: (circle one) 1 2 3 times/day for _____ minutes/hours.**

Compare your answers with the chart above to get a "ballpark" idea of how quickly you can anticipate significant symptom relief. Don't worry or get discouraged if you can't devote as much time as needed to get quick results. If the circumstances of your life constrain your ability to engage in treatment, it's okay. You'll get results; it will just take longer. The most important thing is that you get results. And to do that, you must engage in treatment, even if it takes two or three months. Compared with how long you've suffered these symptoms, a few months is a relatively modest investment to ensure a better future.

The following chart is for you to plan your treatment sessions during the course of the next two months. Make a schedule of your intended treatment days by thinking through which day of the week they will fall on, who you want to be with you, what time of day will work for both of you, competing plans that may need to be rescheduled, etc. This type of planning is difficult, but it will dramatically raise the likelihood of accomplishing your goal of feeling better. Of course, it's not possible to always know with certainty what you will do when. Unexpected things do happen and your schedule will occasionally need modification. But as the old adage says, "Failing to plan is like planning to fail." So create a plan and make it happen.

TREATMENT CALENDAR WORKSHEET

DAY #	DAY OF WEEK	DATE	SUPPORT PERSON WHO WILL BE WITH ME	TRIGGER(S) #	PLANNED TREATMENT TIME	ACTUAL TREATMENT TIME	PLANNED TREATMENT DURATION	ACTUAL TREATMENT DURATION	BEGINNING SUD	ENDING SUD
	Su									
	M									
	T									
	W									
	Th									
	F									
	Sa									
	Su									
	M									
	T									
	W									
	Th									
	F									
	Sa									
	Su									
	M									
	T									
	W									
	Th									
	F									
	Sa									
	Su									
	M									
	T									
	W									
	Th									
	F									
	Sa									

DAY #	DAY OF WEEK	DATE	SUPPORT PERSON WHO WILL BE WITH ME	TRIGGER(S) #	PLANNED TREATMENT TIME	ACTUAL TREATMENT TIME	PLANNED TREATMENT DURATION	ACTUAL TREATMENT DURATION	BEGINNING SUD	ENDING SUD
	Su									
	M									
	T									
	W									
	Th									
	F									
	Sa									
	Su									
	M									
	T									
	W									
	Th									
	F									
	Sa									
	Su									
	M									
	T									
	W									
	Th									
	F									
	Sa									
	Su									
	M									
	T									
	W									
	Th									
	F									
	Sa									

The next tool to help you through each of your ERP treatment sessions is the SUD Recording Chart. Record your SUD score every ten minutes during treatment. The main purposes of this chart are to help you stay focused on your exposure, monitor reductions in your discomfort level, get feedback as to the progress you're making, and assist your brain in rewiring itself.

ERP TREATMENT SESSION RECORDING CHART

DATE: START TIME: TRIGGER #:

MINUTES OF TREATMENT	SUD SCORE
Begin	
10	
20	
30	
40	
50	
60	
70	
80	
90	
100	
110	
120	

DATE: START TIME: TRIGGER #:

MINUTES OF TREATMENT	SUD SCORE
Begin	
10	
20	
30	
40	
50	
60	
70	
80	
90	
100	
110	
120	

DATE: START TIME: TRIGGER #:

MINUTES OF TREATMENT	SUD SCORE
Begin	
10	
20	
30	
40	
50	
60	
70	
80	
90	
100	
110	
120	

DATE: **START TIME:**   **TRIGGER #:**

MINUTES OF TREATMENT	SUD SCORE
Begin	
10	
20	
30	
40	
50	
60	
70	
80	
90	
100	
110	
120	

DATE: **START TIME:**   **TRIGGER #:**

MINUTES OF TREATMENT	SUD SCORE
Begin	
10	
20	
30	
40	
50	
60	
70	
80	
90	
100	
110	
120	

DATE: **START TIME:**   **TRIGGER #:**

MINUTES OF TREATMENT	SUD SCORE
Begin	
10	
20	
30	
40	
50	
60	
70	
80	
90	
100	
110	
120	

DATE: **START TIME:**   **TRIGGER #:**

MINUTES OF TREATMENT	SUD SCORE
Begin	
10	
20	
30	
40	
50	
60	
70	
80	
90	
100	
110	
120	

DATE: START TIME: TRIGGER #:

MINUTES OF TREATMENT	SUD SCORE
Begin	
10	
20	
30	
40	
50	
60	
70	
80	
90	
100	
110	
120	

DATE: START TIME: TRIGGER #:

MINUTES OF TREATMENT	SUD SCORE
Begin	
10	
20	
30	
40	
50	
60	
70	
80	
90	
100	
110	
120	

DATE: START TIME: TRIGGER #:

MINUTES OF TREATMENT	SUD SCORE
Begin	
10	
20	
30	
40	
50	
60	
70	
80	
90	
100	
110	
120	

DATE: START TIME: TRIGGER #:

MINUTES OF TREATMENT	SUD SCORE
Begin	
10	
20	
30	
40	
50	
60	
70	
80	
90	
100	
110	
120	

This agreement specifies the kind of help _____ (support person's name) will provide to me in my plan to conquer OCD. The three main types of support this will provide for me are:

■ **Encouragement.** Know that I am engaging in a self-treatment plan. Ask about my progress. Be willing to talk with me if I am feeling stuck or need help with something specific.

■ **Review.** Everything included in "Encouragement," plus familiarize yourself with the contents of this book. Know the specifics of my treatment plan and understand the written exercises that I choose to share. Be willing to help me think through problem areas in order to design a good program for myself.

■ **Help.** Everything included in "Review," plus actively help me implement my treatment program. Be with me during my ERP treatment sessions when asked. Be familiar with how to refute my automatic negative thoughts and core beliefs. Remind me of my strengths when I waiver. Give me verbal encouragement whenever I need it, but never try to force me to do something I say I'm unwilling to do.

The checked items below are the ones I want help with.

Support person, check the items that you agree to do.

1. Encourage me to complete all the exercises in this book. ☐ ☐

2. Review the exercises with me. ☐ ☐

3. Help me complete the exercises in this book. ☐ ☐

4. Encourage me to develop a personalized ERP plan. ☐ ☐

5. Help me create my personalized ERP plan. ☐ ☐

6. Review my personalized ERP plan. ☐ ☐

7. Encourage me to begin and follow through on my treatment plan. ☐ ☐

8. Help by being with me as I work through the steps of the ERP hierarchy. ☐ ☐

9. Review my progress as I work through the steps of the ERP hierarchy. ☐ ☐

Support Person

It's important also not to do things that help maintain your friend or family member's OCD. Check any of the following that you do.

■ Providing verbal reassurance (e.g., telling the person he or she is okay, doesn't have cancer/AIDS, didn't hurt anyone, is a good person, locked the door, doesn't need to unplug appliances, etc.)

- Washing, laundering, changing clothes, or cleaning things because of the other person's fear of contamination
- Staying out of parts of the house so they don't get "contaminated"
- Putting households objects in their "proper place"
- Making excuses or lying to others about why the other person can't attend gatherings or do things he or she should
- Not being honest with the other person because I think it will cause him or her pain or embarrassment, will start an argument, or will be more work than I have the energy for
- Getting angry with the other person
- Making fun of or teasing the other person

- Being inconsistent or unreliable in my support
- Other: _____

Stopping these behaviors is an important part of the treatment plan. Discuss and write down your plan to stop doing these things so that you and your friend/family member are working together to get him or her better.

_____

_____

_____

_____

_____

This is our agreement for how to end OCD.

_____   _____

OCD sufferer   Support person

Date: _____

Beginning Treatment

At this point, you have all the tools to begin your treatment program. If any of the items in the following list are not complete, it's time to do so.

- ERP Treatment Hierarchy Chart
- **Agreements with your support person/people (see page 131)**
- Treatment calendar
- Imaginal exposure script (if needed)

Begin treatment with your first trigger. You'll rapidly gain experience in the "how to" of ERP. Up until this point it may have seemed a little confusing. But as you do it, you'll get better at it and more willing to tolerate the discomfort of exposure, as well as the fear of treatment itself. Undoubtedly, there will be surprises along the way. Hopefully, they'll be pleasant surprises, but it's often the case that your exposure with response prevention rules may need to be adjusted. This can happen because there were factors you overlooked, forgot about, or may have tried to hide or avoid as you were constructing the rules. That's not uncommon. But as you gain confidence with the process, you can adjust your rules to keep yourself from exposures you're not ready for yet as well as preparing to expose yourself to things you previously couldn't have imagined doing. It takes time, and you'll learn along the way. And like so many other people with OCD who make the effort, you'll get better.

Facing your fear takes courage. You've gotten this far. Now it's time to get started on the part that's really going to pay off: ERP. Begin your treatment sessions and before going on to the following worksheet, Middle Treatment, make sure you've completed at least three treatment sessions.

By now you've completed several treatment sessions and have experienced firsthand the anxiety reduction that occurs with ERP. You've transitioned from ERP being a theoretical idea for treatment to knowing how it works. You know you're capable of tolerating anxiety for longer than you previously thought and have managed to reduce or eliminate your fear of your first few triggers. Congratulations on your success! And you know there's more to be done.

This is a good time to reflect on what you've learned and if necessary make adjustments to your ERP Treatment Hierarchy Chart. It would be very unusual if you had been able to successfully anticipate how ERP would proceed and execute your plan without problems. So it's time to profit from your experience and help your future treatment sessions go more smoothly. The following questions are designed to help you reflect on your experience and improve your next several treatment sessions. As with all the exercises in this book, they only help you if you complete them. Write your answers rather than just think about them. This will force you to think in specifics.

The easiest thing about my first three ERP treatment sessions was ...

The most difficult thing about my first three ERP treatment sessions was ...

The most surprising thing about my first three ERP treatment sessions was ...

If I had it to do over again, I would make the following changes to my ERP treatment plan:

Here's how I intend to improve my next treatment session:

Support person, without looking at the answers above, fill in your own observations below.

For me, the easiest thing about the first three ERP treatment sessions was ...

For me, the most difficult thing about the first three ERP treatment sessions was …

- -

- -

For me, the most surprising thing about the first three ERP treatment sessions was …

- -

- -

If we had it to do over again, I would make the following changes to the ERP treatment plan:

- -

- -

Here's how I think we can improve the next treatment session:

- -

- -

Now compare your responses and discuss what you've learned. Be sure to discuss how to improve your *next* treatment session. Write down specific changes to the exposure with response prevention rules that are needed. If you change your plan, be sure to write your changes down—don't trust yourself to remember them. Update the contract you have with yourself as to how you will conduct ERP.

If you had difficulty thinking of improvements to your treatment plan, consider the following list of possible changes others have made.

- Before beginning my ERP treatment session, use a relaxation technique such as deep breathing or muscle relaxation for several minutes.

- Use a relaxation technique after my ERP session.

- Before I do an actual exposure, use imaginal exposures until my anxiety level doesn't go above 40.

- Devote more time to my ERP session.

- Ask for greater involvement from my support person.

- Be clearer in my instructions to my family and/or support person.

- Write affirmative, encouraging statements to tell myself when I feel like giving up during a treatment session.

- Write down statements I'd like to hear from my support person and give him/her that list so I get the kind of encouragement that works best for me.

- Be more specific as to what fears come automatically to mind, and what each thinking error represents.

- Write longer, more detailed imaginal exposure scripts.

- Listen longer to my imaginal exposure scripts.

- Re-expose myself to the triggers I've already accomplished until they no longer provoke distress.

If any of the above ideas sound useful, incorporate them into your plan. Even if it takes a little more work, do it. This is an investment in yourself that will pay handsome dividends. Revisit this section after every few treatment sessions and continue to modify and improve your plan. Make your treatment plan the best it can be.

Advanced Treatment: The Home Stretch

By this point, you really understand ERP. It's not mysterious any longer. You've gotten over the fear of ERP (even if you're still nervous about exposure to triggers you haven't yet conquered). You're about to expose yourself to items on your treatment hierarchy with SUDs in the 80 to 100 range. What modifications to your plan do you need in order to succeed?

You might need to create additional intermediate exposure steps in your hierarchy prior to tackling the most intense triggers. If that's the case, write the trigger, automatic thoughts, and so forth, along with the needed exposure and response rules. Also, review your suggestions in the Middle Treatment worksheet and continue to tighten up your plan.

You might be ready to keep on going and take on your triggers with the highest SUD ratings. Often, at this point, people can "see the finish line" and are ready to dash on. If that's you, great! Continue to use the tools and techniques that have served you to this point and accomplish your goal.

Also, at this point, it's time to begin planning your ERP Treatment Hierarchy Chart for other obsessions that bother you. If your first hierarchy involved the obsession that bothered you the most, creating another hierarchy should be easy. If you tackled something less than your most time-consuming obsession, you're still well prepared to take on the next challenge and succeed with it, too.

Your toolbox is full of techniques, tricks, tips, and most important . . . successful experiences. Keep going. Nothing leads to success like building on previous success. And if there have been setbacks along the way, they too are full of information about how to fix things to make your future treatment sessions even more successful.

Chapter 10
Healthy Habits

Stretching, Exercise, and Sleep

There are several things you can do to fine-tune your body to help form the foundation for learning anxiety-reduction techniques. Getting enough sound sleep, exercising, and simply learning how to breathe properly are absolutely necessary if you're troubled by anxiety.

Stretching Away the Tension

When you're tense, you may have a tendency to excessively tighten your muscles and inadvertently waste a considerable amount of energy. As you obsess, your anxiety increases, which may make you feel "all wound up" with muscle tension and fatigue. Chronic anxiety builds up in your muscles, making tendons thicken and shorten due to overdevelopment of connective tissue. This tension contributes to the overactivity of the sympathetic nervous system, adding to an already burdened system.

To make matters worse, if you have a sedentary lifestyle you may be even more vulnerable for tension to build up in your body. Because of your lack of movement, your muscles tighten up and atrophy. This tension built up in your body contributes to yet more anxiety. In other words, the tension channels into your body and spills back over into more anxiety because your body "feels tense."

One way you can get rid of this buildup of tension is to stretch. Stretching will drive out tension and relax your muscles. Your muscles are endowed with a rich blood supply, and stretching can promote better blood flow to them, which helps you feel energized and calmer at the same time. By stretching your muscles, you'll force or pump the used and deoxygenated blood back to your lungs for refueling. This blood flow is complemented by the replenishment of reoxygenated blood out to your muscles. Stretching promotes refreshed and invigorated muscles and the release of tension.

Moving to Relax

Exercise is another great way to promote relaxation. It should play a fundamental role in getting your body and brain in balance once again. Exercise produces a "tranquilizing effect." Your underlying anxiety is dampened because of the biochemical changes resulting from physical exertion. It enhances oxygenation of your blood. When blood is transported to your brain, you feel alert and calm.

The many direct and positive benefits of exercise include:

- **Enhanced neurogenesis—new neurons emerge in your hippocampus**
- **Lower pH (increased acidity) of your blood, which increases your energy level**

- Improved circulation (including in your brain)
- Increased oxygenation of your blood and brain, which increases your alertness and ability to concentrate
- Improved digestion, which helps you make better use of the food you eat
- Improved elimination, from your lungs, skin, and bowels
- Improved blood sugar regulation (in the case of hyperglycemia)
- Lower blood pressure (lowering of hypertension)
- Lower cholesterol levels
- Reduced insomnia (especially if done three to six hours before bedtime)
- Weight loss and its vast benefits
- Reduced skeletal muscle tension, which tends to make you feel tense and anxious
- Rechanneling of bottled-up frustration, which can contribute to anxiety
- Burning up of excess adrenaline and thyroxin in your bloodstream, which otherwise would contribute to hypervigilance and tense arousal

There are many ways to exercise. Some involve planning and time commitment; others you can do on the spur of the moment. You can walk or perform other aerobic exercises such as running or bicycle riding almost any time. All of these promote relaxation and a greater sense of well-being.

After vigorous aerobic exercise, many people report a "runner's high." This feeling is the result of the release of the body's endorphins, which are natural brain opiates. Not only do you experience a euphoric and calming feeling after you exercise, but your stress hormones are also reduced.

It can be helpful to structure your exercise into your daily or weekly routine so that it is an expectation—a must. For maximum results you will want to exercise at least once a day.

Although there are no strict rules to suggest that some forms of exercise are better than others, it's best if the exercise:

- Is regular (four or five times per week)
- Is at least twenty to thirty minutes in duration
- Is graduated in intensity (e.g., don't run three miles the first day if you've never run before)
- Includes a warm-up and cooldown; stretching works well for this
- Is aerobic, that is, an activity that gets your heart rate up to the level recommended for your age

Relaxation

Feeling calm may seem like an experience that people without OCD enjoy, but not you. The good news is that you can *learn* to relax and be calm, though it sounds impossible when you are suffering from anxiety. The truth is that you have that capacity built into your body.

As you learned in chapter 4, your autonomic nervous system has two branches: the *sympathetic* nervous system and the *parasympathetic* nervous system. The sympathetic nervous system activates your body, and your parasympathetic nervous system calms it down. In this section, you'll relearn to tap into the talents of your parasympathetic nervous system. Tapping into your parasympathetic branch came naturally earlier in your life. When you developed anxiety, your sympathetic branch came to dominate. Too much activation makes you anxious. Now it's time to get the two branches back into balance. To lower your anxiety, which fuels your OCD, you need to calm down as well as get activated.

Just as there is a balance between your sympathetic and parasympathetic branches, there is also a counterbalance to the fight-or-flight response. Dubbed the *relaxation response* by Harvard professor Herbert Benson, it is your body's parasympathetic nervous system in action. It helps lower your heart rate and metabolism and slow down your breathing rate.

For thousands of years, people in societies all over the world have developed ways to induce the relaxation response and activate the parasympathetic nervous system without even knowing of their existence. Techniques have been developed to cultivate a state of calmness and spirituality. Referred to as prayer and meditation, these techniques were devised to cultivate a sense of inner peace. Although the names and terminology are different, they are based on the same principles and the same physiology.

Seven Principles of Relaxation

There are seven elements common to many forms of prayer, meditation, relaxation exercises, and hypnosis. They include:

1. **Breathing rhythmically.** Deep, deliberate, and focused breathing allows you to slow your heartbeat and to center your attention on relaxation.

2. **Focused attention.** Because much of anxiety is nervous anticipation of the future, by gently focusing your attention on the here and now you can transform each moment into a rich and calm experience in the present. This activates your frontal lobes to focus their attention and exert their ability to inhibit the overreactivity of your amygdala. Some practices include a "point focus"—meaning you focus on one word, such as a mantra, or on breathing. This and principle 6 in this list are part of the "O" in ORDER.

3. **A quiet environment.** This will give you an opportunity to learn how to relax without distractions. Later, during times when you cannot go to a quiet environment, you can practice the relaxation that you learned earlier while in a more serene environment.

4. **An accepting and a nonjudgmental attitude.** By shifting away from rigid expectations to an accepting attitude, you'll come to appreciate reality as it is, rather than what you fear it could be. This will free you to adjust to whatever happens. When you let yourself experience the here and now instead of fearing the future, you'll be more relaxed and present.

5. **A relaxed posture.** This can include sitting in a relaxed position or stretching.

6. **Observation.** This allows you to detach from anxiety while not denying its existence. As you observe your experience nonjudgmentally, you can simply note what is occurring at any one time. The vantage point of being the observer, instead of being the victim, allows you to distance yourself from the anxiety.

7. **Labeling what you experience.** Labeling accesses your left frontal lobe and its positive emotions. In other words, you call OCD symptoms what they are. This works if you remain in an accepting and nonjudgmental attitude as a detached observer. This principle is also part of the "R" in ORDER.

The principles detailed on the previous page can help you lower your anxiety by "letting go" of sympathetic nervous system arousal. Each of the principles by themselves helps defuse anxiety, and when combined they are particularly powerful in putting you at ease. When you shift your attention to accepting and observing the present moment while simultaneously breathing deeply, for example, the situations that you had previously associated with anxiety can now be experienced with a relaxed attitude.

One final concept needs to be considered now before moving on to the exercises. Because trying "too hard" to relax will actually make you more stressed, letting go of sympathetic arousal by widening your attention allows your body (through the parasympathetic nervous system) to calm down. Widening your attention means that you focus on other things in addition to trying to relax, such as the weight of your arms or the lightness of your breath. The concept of letting go of trying hard can be counterintuitive. If you try too hard to relax, you will probably stay tense. By *allowing* yourself to relax instead of *trying* to relax, you lower the tension so that you can relax.

The Progressive Relaxation Method

You might want to try a traditional and very popular relaxation technique called *progressive relaxation*. It involves tensing and releasing particular muscle groups such as your fingers or toes while simultaneously breathing deeply. Don't tense too hard—just enough to feel the tension, and don't rush through this as if it were an aerobic exercise.

Start by splaying your toes and keeping the muscles in your feet tense. After you count to ten, release the muscles. Notice and enjoy the flow of relaxation for at least twenty seconds. Work your way in this manner up your body, area by area. Tense and relax the same muscle three times for the same period of time followed by the same relaxation period.

Imagery

Your imagination can be a powerful tool to calm your anxiety and temper your obsessions and compulsions. Because you use it every day for periodic daydreaming, you might as well make it work for you instead of against you. Don't forget that you're both the scriptwriter and the main actor here. Have fun with it and make it a calming experience.

Just as you may imagine bad experiences if you don't engage in compulsive behaviors, you can instead imagine positive experiences. For this reason, imagery is a relaxation technique that has gained popularity over the past thirty years for treatment of not only anxiety but also health concerns. You can use your imagination to enhance what you do at work or on personal projects. For example, imagine yourself achieving an ambitious goal at work, and then concentrate on doing things that approach that goal.

Meditation and Prayer

One of the most comprehensive and powerful ways to shift your attention and calm yourself is through meditation and prayer. Most religions have literature, including manuals, on meditation or prayer. Within Hinduism, Buddhism, Sufism, Judaism, and Christianity, meditation and/or prayer have a long tradition and have been practiced for thousands of years. The practitioners generally had pious intentions and the psychological benefits were not well known. By the twentieth century, the effects of meditation and prayer were thoroughly researched and found to have a wide range of positive and healthy benefits, including anxiety reduction.

Most types of meditation involve allowing your mind to clear while focusing on your breathing. Clearing your mind can be accomplished by concentrating on a few words, referred to as a mantra, such as "sat nam." For example, you say the word *sat* on every inhalation and the word *nam* on the exhalations. As you concentrate on the mantra and your breath, your mind clears and your body relaxes. Meditation and prayer are embraced by most religious traditions because there is thought to be great value in attempting to lose petty personal problems and appreciating a wider consciousness by shifting your attention beyond personal concerns. As you focus on a broader reality, and the fact that you are but a small part of a greater whole, you detach from your day-to-day worries.

Prayer, too, when practiced not to achieve some reward, achieves the same benefits. When you pray simply to be closer to God, you promote a deep sense of inner peace. Many methods of praying involve repeating a phrase or entire verses, such as the Lord's Prayer. Like mantras, these phrases serve to help you direct your attention away from your obsessions as long as you don't get obsessional about it!

Chapter 11

Health Obsessions

Both of us work within the largest full-service and integrated health care system in the United States. We are in constant contact with primary care physicians, dermatologists, cardiologists, and so on. A topic that often comes up is patients who either obsess about or imagine a medical problem and are forever distressed and worried about present or possible future health issues.

If you are one of these people, you may have constant obsessive worries about a specific health concern. These obsessions may center on a particular physical sensation or a wide variety of physical complaints. The most common ones include:

- Headaches
- Gastrointestinal distress
- Back pain
- Breathing irregularities
- Rapid heartbeat
- Fatigue
- Insomnia

In this chapter, you'll learn how obsessions about health concerns can snowball into a career as a chronic patient when you actually have a minor physical problem or no problem at all. You'll also learn how to focus on being healthy instead of being ill. Finally, you'll learn to make healthy habits your prescription for the treatment of health obsessions.

Making Molehills Out of Molehills

Instead of making mountains out of molehills, your goal here is to practice the ERP part of the ORDER method to keep molehills simply molehills. To this end, it will be useful to learn how molehills can inadvertently become mountains.

How and where you focus your attention plays a large role in what you experience. If you are worried about a particular physical sensation, even if that sensation is not a symptom of a true medical problem, it can become a source of increasingly greater concern.

The degree of worry you devote to that sensation may actually intensify it. For example, you may pay such close attention to the mild symptoms of a headache that you make your experience of those symptoms more intense. This potential for making mountains out of molehills is multiplied if you have fundamental thinking errors, including black and white thinking, catastrophizing, and pessimism.

Let's focus on black and white thinking as an example of how you can inadvertently intensify physical sensations and as a result feel them more intensely. If you have a tendency to obsess about stomach pain, you look out for any indication that stomach pain is on the way. Any feeling coming from your stomach turns on the alarm and you say to yourself, "Oh no, here it comes!" This false alarm activates your amygdala and the fear circuit with its fight-or-flight response mechanisms, which increases the anxiety by activating neurotransmitters such as norepinephrine and epinephrine (adrenaline), which increase the symptoms of a nervous stomach. This is all you need!

A similar sequence can occur when there is no initial stomach condition. If you believe that you have a stomach condition, you'll be extremely attentive to any feeling in or near your stomach. The reality is, everyone has feelings in their midsection. You will inevitably find stomach sensations if you look for them. To compound this obsessional search for stomach sensations, your reaction to those sensations when you find them can intensify them. Your fear circuit gets activated and the resulting physical sensations will intensify as your sympathetic nervous system arousal mechanisms become hyperactive.

Too often, people who are obsessed about their health forget that their obsessive concerns and compulsive checking behaviors are a vicious cycle. If you are obsessed about your health, why not put those con-

Medication Quicksand

We are fortunate to work within a highly integrated medical system that minimizes misdiagnosis and maximizes coordinated treatment. For example, one of us (DD) heads up the behavioral medicine team that works within the medicine departments to treat psychologically-caused medical problems. However, we aren't perfect. Because primary care physicians have to deal daily with ever greater numbers of patients seeking timely treatment, occasionally OCD patients who complain about physical sensations and/or psychologically-based medical problems, such as headaches or abdominal pain, receive "treatment" for these "medical problems."

Too often, even in our integrated system, the doctor prescribes a pain or an antianxiety medication. Once medication such as benzodi-azepines or synthetic opiates is introduced, a vicious cycle starts, which involves the phenomena of tolerance and withdrawal. As time passes, higher dosages are needed to get the same pain-reducing effect. During the withdrawal phase, there is an increase in symptoms because of complex biochemical processes that involve reduced production of key neurotransmitters. As a result of this spiral, the headaches and/or other pains increase. This increase in pain often results in another decision to increase the dosage to get this same "pain reducing" effect. To make matters worse, benzodiazepines and synthetic opiates are addictive. This medication quicksand only serves to increase the pain/headaches syndrome that may have begun as a minor annoyance.

cerns to good use by adopting healthier habits? Don't be like Penny, who, despite her concerns, actually did things that made her condition worse when she thought she was making it better.

Penny's Ritual

Penny was referred to us after admitting to her primary care physician that she spent an hour each day trying to prepare herself for the day so that she would not be tormented by headaches. Her headaches started around 10:30 each morning and lasted until sometime after lunch.

When she was asked what she did to prepare herself in the morning, she said, "I get up and try to calm myself with a little tea ceremony." She went on to describe in meticulous detail how she learned the tea ceremony in Japan when she was an exchange student, and how in recent years she had embellished it by counting as she poured her cups of tea.

When asked how many cups, she said that she had four cups every morning, and then she had lunch at 12:35 p.m.

"So you skip breakfast?"

"Oh, yes. I'm just too nauseous in the morning to eat. The tea helps settle my stomach."

"Black tea?"

She nodded. "Oolong."

After she was told that black tea contains not only caffeine but also tannic acid, which doesn't settle the stomach but rather irritates the lining, she looked alarmed. To make matters worse, consuming that amount of caffeine stimulated the sympathetic branch of her autonomic nervous system, which resulted in heightened feelings of anxiety that only aggravated any abdominal distress. She was also informed that by skipping breakfast she was depleting her store of neurotransmitters that could help her deal with the stomach pain and lower her anxiety level.

"But I don't have an appetite in the morning. What about the wisdom of my body that tells me what is right for it?"

"Your body wants less pain and distress, right? Eating breakfast before or, better yet, instead of drinking tea would help it get what it wants."

If you, like Penny, are not practicing healthy habits, such as proper nutrition, and instead are doing things that contribute to the very physical problem that torments you, it's time to get back on track.

Use the following worksheet to assess and monitor your healthy habits. Jot down any physical complaints week by week and the bad habits that may contribute to them. The physical complaints should fade as you also note what you are doing about them and the corresponding SUD scores. Notice how your SUD score is abnormally high. Next, jot down how you are going to change the bad habit and develop a healthy habit.

PHYSICAL COMPLAINT	BAD HABIT THAT MAY CONTRIBUTE TO IT	SUD SCORE	PLAN FOR CHANGE

Gaining ORDER Out of Physical Complaints

In our medical system, the practice of mindfulness (part of the observation step of the ORDER method) has been a key component of the treatment of serious medical problems, such as chronic pain. You may wonder why a medical center promotes observing physical pain as a viable way to treat it. Wouldn't we want to avoid chronic pain by trying to put it out of our mind at all costs? The simple but paradoxical answer is no. This is a paradox because the more you try to force pain out of your mind, the more that pain demands attention.

An example of how this paradox works goes something like this: Try hard to get pink flamingos out of your mind! The more you try to keep any image or thought of pink flamingos from your mind, the more they will pop into it. A funny thing happens, on the other hand, when you observe and accept the thought of pink flamingos: they fade away. Observing and accepting thoughts of pink flamingos takes the negative charge associated with them away, so those images can fade into the background.

If you are dealing with chronic pain by trying not to think of it, the same paradox occurs: You can't force the pain out of your mind. When you try, the pain gets worse. It's better to accept the pain—then it fades into the background. Next you incorporate the reminding step. This means reminding yourself that the last time you suffered a bout of pain you survived it despite having previously catastrophized

about it. Reminders like this help you lower the anxiety associated with the pain and as result lessen the pain itself.

The doing step of ORDER means that you just don't sit around; you engage in something pleasurable. People in our chronic pain programs are encouraged to expand their activities, not contract them. Rather than withdraw into the role of being a patient who is so overwhelmed by pain that they think normal activities are no longer possible, they are encouraged to do things that give them joy and a sense that life is worth living. What happens if they say initially (as they often do) that they are in too much pain to enjoy anything? If they don't do anything, they can't possibly enjoy anything. They simply sit at home suffering from chronic pain. One rebuttal to that negativistic thinking error is this: Let's say you go to the movies and only get ten minutes of enjoyment from a ninety-minute movie. That's ten minutes of enjoyment you would not have had if you'd stayed home suffering.

Doing something instead of centering your life around a physical problem (real or imagined) is critical for your health. Doing something enjoyable activates body and brain resources as a positive alternative to obsessing about your physical problem.

The exposure phase of dealing with obsessions about health problems is perhaps the most difficult to grasp. As with the observation step, you may wonder why you would want to expose yourself to pain or a health problem. The answer to that question involves the paradoxical and destructive effect of avoidance. Remember the pink flamingo effect? Exposure is the opposite of avoidance. With chronic pain, for example, you can't perform your observations unless you expose yourself to what you fear so that you can eventually habituate to it.

Finally, response prevention involves making sure that you don't do what you have habitually done in the past, such as reach for the pain medication to escape exposure to pain. One of the common compulsive behaviors associated with health-related obsessions is going to the doctor and requesting medical tests you don't need just so that you can be reassured that you don't have the disease you're obsessing about. Unfortunately, when you engage in checking behaviors like these you keep getting brief periods of "relief." But eventually going to the doctor all the time will result in the "boy who cried wolf" phenomenon. You want your doctor to take you seriously, so ask for help only when you really need help.

Rather than engaging in your old compulsive behavior, practice the other steps in the ORDER method. As you can see, these steps are not sequential but meant to be practiced simultaneously. When you do so, ORDER promotes healthy behavior as well as physical health.

Sadie's Crack in the Door

Sadie came in to see one of us after her primary care physician became frustrated that she was a "frequent flyer"—meaning that she demanded excessive medical examinations, far more than the normal patient. The first thing out of her mouth was, "I know he thinks it's all in my head. He won't listen to me." When she was asked if there was any possibility that some (though not all) of it was, she responded quickly, "How could some of it be in my head?"

She was told how extreme anxiety about physical problems often intensifies the symptoms because the body is put in a hyperalert.

"It is a walking nightmare, living with this constant stomach pain," she answered.

"Could it be that having to live with that nightmare makes you anxious?"

"Well, yeah, wouldn't you be anxious?"

"Sure. What if some of that anxiety makes your body so tense and hypersensitive that your stomach condition gets worse?"

"But what am I supposed to do about that?"

"Maybe we can teach you some coping techniques."

She shrugged her shoulders.

Over the next several weeks Sadie learned some coping techniques, including relaxation exercises. During that same period of time she did not ask for one visit to her primary care physician. When this was pointed out to her, she responded, "Oh, is that all you people care about?"

"Actually, no. It's seeing you so much more relaxed and healthy that is important."

Her demeanor returned to its recently acquired relaxed state. "These last few weeks have been a sort of vacation."

"Would you want to work together to extend that vacation?"

She nodded tearfully.

If you, like Sadie, go to your doctor with obsessive physical complaints that really amount to compulsive checking behavior, then you're actually contributing to your distress. More important, you're increasing your anxiety level, which carries over to an increase in your physical distress.

HEALTH CHECKING BEHAVIORS MONITORING WORKSHEET

Use the following worksheet to monitor your health obsessions and compulsive checking behaviors. Jot down your physical complaint and your SUD score in response to that physical complaint. Then jot down your compulsive checking behavior associated with that physical complaint. Next, note the SUD score right after the checking behavior. Next note the time that elapses before your obsessions about your health go back up, as measured by the rise in your SUD score. And note the SUD score. The purpose of this worksheet is to illustrate that the checking behaviors actually contribute to a vicious cycle, which makes you more prone to obsess about your health.

PHYSICAL COMPLAINT	SUD SCORE 1–100	CHECKING BEHAVIORS	SUD SCORE 1–100	TIME ELAPSED	SUD SCORE 1–100

Notice how your SUD score goes down briefly after your checking behavior, only to go back up before long. It's a vicious cycle that needs to be broken so that your distress can go down permanently.

Use the following worksheet to chart how your distress goes down as you refrain from engaging in the checking behaviors. First jot down your physical complaint and your SUD score. Then implement the ORDER. Finally, jot down your SUD score after implementing the ORDER. Follow this procedure each time you obsess about your health.

HEALTH CHECKING BEHAVIORS ORDER WORKSHEET

PHYSICAL COMPLAINT	SUD SCORE 1–100	ORDER	SUD SCORE 1–100

Edgar's Roving Concerns

Edgar initially went to his doctor's office to "get a brain scan." He was convinced that he had a brain tumor. His primary care physician told him that his symptoms did not indicate that he had a tumor. Nevertheless, Edgar demanded a CAT scan and added, "I'm paying for this health insurance and you can't deny my treatment. That would be malpractice."

Against his better judgment, his primary care physician ordered a CAT scan. When the results came back he sat down with Edgar and reported, "It looks like you're clear. No signs of a tumor."

"That can't be! You must be missing something. Why didn't you do an MRI? They're much more precise."

The primary care physician knew he had a patient who could get litigious if he didn't follow through on the request, so he ordered an MRI. When those results too came back negative, Edgar again was frustrated, saying, "Why can't you people find it?"

"Maybe because it doesn't exist."

"But what about my headaches?" Edgar asked incredulously.

"Maybe one of our psychologists can help you learn to cope with them."

"So you think I'm crazy?" he said, looking dejected.

Edgar showed up for his first therapy appointment still reeling from his argument with his primary care physician.

To initially allay his fears, he was told that our job wouldn't be to discover whether or not he was "crazy," but to help him learn some relaxation techniques to lessen the intensity of his headaches. That plan, Edgar admitted, sounded reasonable. Yet, he asked, "Please talk to my doctor so that he takes me seriously." Edgar learned various relaxation techniques over the course of the next few weeks. He experienced fewer and less intense headaches as a result.

A funny thing occurred on his fourth visit. He said, "I think the disease went to my stomach." He went on to describe how he no longer suffered from headaches but now had abdominal pain. "I've been reading up on these problems and I don't think I had a brain tumor. The headaches were just an early symptom of a stomach disease. Please do a blood workup. I need to be properly treated."

He was invited to reflect on the fact that he was almost symptom-free before this totally new stomach symptom emerged. "Perhaps this has less to do with an actual physical disorder and more to do with your tendency to search for one." In fact, it was discovered that over the prior weekend he had eaten a sandwich with some mayonnaise that had been left unrefrigerated for too long. Although it was short of actual food poisoning, he did experience some gastrointestinal distress. The next day he continued his intense hyper-vigilance of potential gastrointestinal distress, which raised his anxiety and increased his "nervous stomach."

For the first time, Edgar experienced an insightful breakthrough. The fact that his primary focus was now his stomach instead of his head added to the credibility of OCD being the disorder he should be looking for instead of a physical disease. Over the course of the next few months, he was taught to use the ORDER method. To his delight, his obsessions decreased while his quality of life increased.

Chapter 12

Help for Hoarding

Hoarding is a unique type of OCD. It is estimated that between 18 and 31 percent of people with OCD are hoarders. If you are a hoarder, you may refer to yourself as a "collector" or a "shopaholic" or a "saver." Others may call you a "pack rat" or a "junk collector." No matter what your nickname, you probably save such things as newspapers, magazines, empty boxes, junk mail, old clothing, food wrappers, and books that you may never read nor that interest you (but you save them just in case you may develop those interests some day).

Your home may be so cluttered and messy that there's scarcely a place to put anything without it getting lost in the chaos. If you have a spouse, s/he is far more concerned about the clutter than you are. If s/he tries to get rid of a few things, you probably get pretty upset.

There is reason for hope. The fact that you are reading this chapter puts you far ahead of most hoarders. Generally speaking, they are quite resistant to change. Getting hoarding out of your life can be difficult, but it is certainly doable if you follow the steps in this chapter. You'll learn how to get rid of not just the debris but also the compulsion to "collect" more things. Once you start shedding the junk from your life and resist the temptation to collect more, you'll feel liberated.

There are some risk factors that may make you more vulnerable to hoarding. These include:

- **Family history—If you have close family relatives who were hoarders**
- **Social isolation—If you have withdrawn from others, you may turn to the comfort of hoarding**
- **Stressful life event—If you have had a stressful life event, such as the loss of a loved one or a divorce**

Collecting or Hoarding?

A little discriminate collecting does not constitute hoarding and OCD. It's the degree of collecting and how it affects your life that identifies a hoarder. It will be useful to take a look at how and to what degree hoarding affects your life. Answer the following questions:

Do your family members call you a "pack rat"?. . . . . Y N

Is there so much clutter in your house that it's hard to see what is valuable and what is trash?. . . . . Y N

Do you find it difficult to throw things away? . . . . . . Y N

Is your house cluttered with your collections? . . . . . Y N

Do you bring home useless things?. . . . . Y N

Do people tell you that you are a "scavenger"? . . . Y N

Does it bother you when other people touch your possessions? . . . . Y N

Do you keep things because you might need them many years from now? . . . . Y N

Are you very possessive of the things you own? . . . Y N

Are people always telling you to clear out that debris? . . . . Y N

Does it take you longer to do things than other people? . . . . Y N

Have your "collections" contributed to a feeling of being overwhelmed? . . . . Y N

Are you ashamed to invite people over to your home? . . . . Y N

Is it hard to find a place to sit down at home? . . . . Y N

Do you save used food containers? . . . . Y N

Do you have more pets than you can realistically care for? . . . . Y N

Are you more attached to possessions than most people are? . . . . Y N

Would you become anxious if you had to get rid of things? . . . . Y N

Do others encourage you to get professional help? . . . . Y N

Do you procrastinate about doing chores or discarding things? . . . . Y N

If you answered "yes" to two or more of the questions above, there is serious reason to be concerned about hoarding and to do the exercises in this chapter. You probably use all sorts of rationalizations for your behaviors. Do you find yourself saying such things as:

"This is too good to throw away." . . . . Y N

"I might need this later." . . . . Y N

"This should not be wasted.". . . . . Y N

"This is important information." . . . . Y N

"I'm going to save this for _____." . . . . Y N

"I better keep this, just in case _____." . . . . . . Y N

"Maybe I should save this for my kids." . . . . Y N

"When in doubt, save it and decide later." . . . . Y N

If the statements above ring a bell for you, it's time to make some changes. Yet, it's one thing to say you need to do something about your hoarding and another to do it. The question you'll need to ask yourself is, "Am I ready to do what it takes to get rid of my excess stuff even if it makes me *very* anxious?" Another way to look at this is to ask yourself, "Is there more to be gained by getting rid of some junk?" Another important question is, "What am I losing by holding on to all this clutter?"

The answer to the second question helps answer the first. For example:

LOSING	GAINING
I can't invite people over now.	I can have friends over without shame.
I lose things in the clutter.	I can find what I need.
The clutter makes me depressed.	I feel liberated by seeing my space.
I feel bad about myself.	I feel much better about myself.
I hate the way my house looks.	I enjoy my house again.
The clutter makes it hard to do things.	With the clutter gone I can get things done easily.
My spouse is angry because of the clutter.	My spouse and I get along much better now.

The last of these lose/win factors is quite common. For example, Celina came in for help only after her husband complained that he would leave her unless she got rid of all the clutter. He said, "It's either get rid of the junk or I leave."

This threat put her into a tailspin. It was one thing to put a halt to all the collecting. That was difficult enough, but to get rid of everything she had collected seemed next to impossible. Where would she start? How could she start? She even considered giving up the marriage to hold on to her possessions. Sure, she understood that her husband was frustrated because it was hard to find a place to sit down for dinner because both the kitchen and the dining room tables were cluttered with stuff. She wasn't actually sure what was in the piles, but it seemed like it all was important. What if she needed some of it later?

She used all these justifications with her husband. He wasn't the slightest bit receptive to any of her rationalizations. So she came in and tried them on us. Again, no luck. She had answered yes to five of the previous questions on hoarding and realized that it was time to do something about her hoarding problem. Maybe there was more to be gained than lost.

As you learned in chapter 5, there are some fundamental thinking errors that contribute to OCD. With hoarding, there are some unique ones that make it difficult to get rid of the things you have accumulated and to resist accumulating more. Researchers have identified five main thinking errors in people who have problems with hoarding. Do you suffer from one or all of the following?

- **Excessive emotional attachment to things.** You may think of your "stuff" as part of you. Consequently, the thought of getting rid of some of it may feel threatening, as if losing a part of yourself.
- **Fear of memory problems.** You may worry that if you put something "out of sight" it may go "out

of mind," and therefore be forgotten. Your concern about your memory may motivate you not to put things away, which inadvertently leads to clutter.

- **Exaggerated need for control of belongings.** You may have a very strong need to control the things that you have collected. When someone moves them or even touches them, you may feel personally violated.

- **Indecision.** You may tend to have a great deal of difficulty making decisions even about what to have for dinner or what to wear for the day. Consequently, when it comes to objects, you don't want to make the "wrong" decision and get rid of something only to regret it later.

- **Categorization problems.** You may have a great deal of difficulty sorting through things and knowing what to keep and what to discard. For example, you may save a ticket stub from a movie you went to three years ago and newspapers from five years ago. This difficulty in differentiating what is important and valuable from what is unimportant and useless makes your accumulation of useless stuff compound.

These thinking errors add up to an OCD trap. The excessive emotional attachment to stuff that you feel now can be transformed into a realistic and forward-thinking way to deal with that stuff. For example, if you are so emotionally attached to your stuff, then you need to ask yourself why you are treating it so carelessly, why you have it cluttered up in disorganized piles if you care so much for it. Why not honor it by organizing it and taking care of it better?

If you are worried about your memory and therefore fail to put things away because you are worried that you can't find them later, think again. Ask yourself. "Can I find anything now?" In fact, if you are really worried about "out of sight, out of mind," why put your things in a clutter? Do you really know where to find things now in all of this? Thus, if you're worried about your memory, you'll need to clear out the clutter.

If you have an exaggerated need to control your belongings, then why lose control of your things in the clutter? Ask yourself if you really feel in control of your things now. You'll be in far better control if you know where things are and that they are placed in organized locations so that they can be accessible.

Because indecision has played such a significant role in your hoarding, you need to confront it head-on. If you are concerned about making the wrong decision, then think of how much more complicated you are making that decision by allowing things to pile up.

Because problems with categorizing lead to cluttering, you'll need to ask yourself "what" you are actually hoarding. And because you seem to value what you are hoarding, it's important to also ask yourself "why." By forcing yourself to answer these questions, you'll also force yourself to exercise your categorizing skills.

Follow these guidelines to help correct the thinking errors that fuel your hoarding.

PROBLEM	EXERCISE
Categorization	Ask yourself what is so important about each thing you are tempted to hoard.
Indecisiveness	Give yourself five minutes, and then choose the best option no matter what it is.
Worries about memory	Do an inventory of your belongings.
Control of ownership	Invite love ones to share ownership.

Letting Go and Saying No

Imagine trying to bail out a sinking boat with a bucket while water gushes in the hole in the hull at a greater rate than your feeble attempt to bail. This is what can happen if you make only a partial effort to deal with your hoarding.

Thus, there are two fundamental problems that you'll need to confront:

- **Stopping the accumulation of things that add up to clutter**
- **Deciding what to do with the existing clutter**

Ground Rules

Because it can seem overwhelming to deal with the dual problem of your collecting habit and getting rid of the clutter you've already collected, setting ground rules as to how you will deal with it can help make you feel less overwhelmed.

1. **Enact a moratorium.** You'll need to stop collecting before you get rid of what you collected. This will put pressure on you to get rid of your clutter. You can do this by placing a moratorium on new stuff coming in until there is *room* and *reason*. The room part of this equation means that the clutter has to be gone before you bring more stuff in. The reason part is that there has to be a good reason for it to come in (we'll explain this one in more detail later).

2. **Pace yourself.** Because getting rid of all the clutter is a long-range goal that will take time, you'll need to pace yourself. You can't get it all done in one day, or perhaps even one week. On the other hand, you'll need to hold yourself accountable for getting a certain amount done each day, or every few days. In fact, you can break down the day into thirty- or sixty-minute chunks. Alternate de-cluttering

periods with thirty- or sixty-minute breaks to do something enjoyable.

3. **Label boxes.** By setting things up to aid you with categorizing, you'll make the process of getting rid of things much more manageable. Label boxes "donate," "give away," "sell," "throw away," and "recycle." The labeled boxes will help you sort through your stuff. We recommend that every time you fill a box you take it away.

4. **Go room by room.** Instead of trying to tackle the whole house and garage all together, which will get you sidetracked and overwhelmed, pick one room and finish it before going on to the next. We recommend starting with the heavy traffic rooms first, such as the kitchen and the family room, so that you can see and enjoy the fruits of your labors.

5. **Handle something only once.** To cut through indecision, use the following maxim: "Only handle it once." The acronym OHIO can help you remember this. This means that once you touch an item or pick it up, don't put it down in an indecisive pile. Place it in one of the labeled boxes. If you can't decide which box to put it in, use this rule: "When in doubt, get rid of it." This rule should be your default mode because your problem has been holding on to things that should have been gotten rid of right away. If they are new items, bought but never used, donate them. This will give you a sense of satisfaction knowing that someone will find a good use for them.

6. **Make sure that cleared space remains cleared space.** Once you have conquered a space, make sure that it stays uncluttered and fully usable for what it was intended for. For example, a dining room table is where you eat, so make sure it remains clear for only that purpose. This will also give you the opportunity to look back and enjoy your accomplishments. Think of each conquered area as a beachhead, a liberated and unclutttered area.

7. **Don't get sidetracked by so-called emergencies.** There will always be false emergencies that can distract you. Stay focused on your de-cluttering work. Consider the time that you work on de-cluttering as your primary agenda.

8. **Reward yourself with sensible rewards.** Once you have cleared your house of the clutter, you can reward yourself by carefully selecting things you *need* in the future. Don't buy or collect anything that you "think" you may need. Think of the "free space" as healthy space. Cluttered space is dead space or cancer that can grow. Keep your life clean and healthy. For everything new you bring into the house, get rid of two items. If it is a book, get rid of two before buying the new book, and spend at least a half hour with it at the bookstore before buying it.

9. **Do first things first.** As you get rid of the clutter, be sure to take care of yourself. Your personal hygiene is a fundamental need. If, for example, your tub or shower has possessions piled up in it, you'll

need to move that stuff out as soon as possible. Your nutrition is also a fundamental need. If you can't use your stove or refrigerator to cook or get access to food, you'll need to move that stuff as soon as possible. Another need that you should address immediately is "social medicine." Because social isolation can get you depressed and make your hoarding worse, you'll need to rebuild your social contacts.

Janet's Liberation

Janet had been hoarding for so long she wasn't sure when it all started. She always considered herself a perfectionist but had also been troubled by indecision. She wanted to be ready to respond to any audit, give someone an article that she thought was important, and have a supply of little gifts available to give people. Unfortunately, she couldn't decide what was worth keeping and what wasn't.

Consequently, things piled up. She didn't know that it had gotten so bad until her kids complained that she had always told them to clean up when she had the biggest mess. Then her daughter added, "You don't know that you drove Dad off with this mess!"

She had never wanted to cause her daughter any problems. She wanted to provide her daughter with a good home, and now the obvious was obvious even to her daughter. She somehow had hoped her daughter would never notice, and she herself was trying not to notice it. Her husband had decided he couldn't live like that anymore, and now she vowed to do something about it so that her daughter wouldn't have to.

Yet, actually getting started was difficult. Just the thought of getting started spurred a panic attack.

Janet came in for help initially asking that we help her "patch up the problem" with her daughter. She was still in denial about how her hoarding was affecting her daughter. Her daughter was still upset about the divorce and was threatening to go live with her father. When asked why the marriage ended, Janet tried to change the subject. When redirected back to the question she admitted that her "collections" were a "sore spot."

A key point, therefore, in kindling motivation for de-cluttering was the loss of her most important relationship. Although that loss made her feel more anxiety and despair about losing her "collections" too, the bottom line was that she was going to experience anxiety either way. She decided that there was more to lose by trying to hold on to her collections.

She agreed with the moratorium on acquiring new things, knowing that she had no more room to stack things anyway. She understood that her task was to approach this methodically, pacing herself as she attacked the rooms one by one.

Her first target was the kitchen, and she began with the kitchen table. Her daughter was as pleased as she was to sit down to dinner at a table that was clear of everything but the food that they shared. After she finished de-cluttering the kitchen, she compared the before and after photos and was amazed with her accomplishment.

With renewed vigor and confidence, she moved on to the next worksheet and room. As she started on the family room, continuing to follow the ground rules, she felt increasingly liberated. The praise and encouragement from her daughter was frosting on the cake.

Chapter 13

Prevent Relapse with ORDER-ABC

Because you've worked hard to learn how to minimize OCD, you'll want to make sure that these gains last. To ensure that they actually do last, you'll need to keep with ORDER. This means practicing the ORDER skills regularly.

Repetition is critical for the neuroplasticity that rewires your brain and instills new habits. If you fall back into old patterns, you'll rekindle the well-worn neural networks that bring back your obsessions and compulsions. Think of OCD as a bad habit that you want only as a distant memory. In this chapter, you'll learn how to prevent relapse.

Managing Setbacks

Your progress will be tested by stress or even laziness. This is when repeating the ORDER method is most critical. Let's say that you are doing well for several months and your OCD symptoms fade away. Then you experience some major stress, such as a move to a new home or a layoff from your job. Your anxiety goes up, which triggers the old feelings that you remember are of when you engaged in your OCD behaviors. Your amygdala again signals, "Alarm! Alarm!" You want to make sure that you respond to this alarm with healthy behaviors rather than OCD ones. Thus, repeating the ORDER steps is all the more important. You want your healthy coping behavior to be the default mode, rather than your old OCD reactions. This is a pivotal point. If you fall back on your old behaviors, you will rekindle the OCD circuits in your brain. If, on the other hand, you continue to repeat the steps of the new ORDER, you'll rewire your brain.

It's common to experience brief periods of obsessional thinking during and after the recovery process because almost no one is anxiety-free, and your obsessional thinking had been triggered by anxiety in the past. People often get so excited about their progress in overcoming OCD that they gravitate back to thinking errors, such as all-or-nothing thinking. Fueled by enthusiasm, they assume that they have been "cured" and that they are completely free of OCD. Once they've made this thinking error, they're at risk of experiencing minor setbacks with periods of disturbing anxiety and falling back into their old pattern of obsessions and compulsive behaviors. What was once a little anxiety becomes OCD. Now they go to the other extreme and assume that they are back to full-blown

OCD, that all the progress they made is lost, and that they have to start all over again. Worse, some people then think of themselves as incapable of making *any* long-term progress. The following are some of the common overreactions to setbacks:

- "I was incapable of making it last."
- "This must mean that my anxiety problem is worse than I thought."
- "After all the work I've done, I'm right back where I started."
- "I guess the gains I made were all superficial."
- "Why try if I'm just going to fall back again?"
- "All those ORDER techniques weren't for people with real OCD like mine."
- "I can't change my OCD genes."
- "Everything I've done is lost now, and I can't climb back up."
- "All those ORDER techniques were just Band-Aids on top of a compound fracture."
- "My mother taught me how to be obsessive, and I guess I'll never shake it."
- "I've got a rare medical problem and everyone is wrong that's it's all in my imagination."
- "This relapse proves I have bad brain chemistry."
- "I guess my brain is too damaged."
- "God will never forgive me."

Setbacks are opportunities to learn lessons. They remind you that you weren't practicing your ORDER skills and that there's still work to be done. They let you know that you have not been following the plan, or not following it consistently. Following are some realistic responses to a setback:

- "I better practice my ORDER techniques more often."
- "I was getting out of practice."
- "Whoops. I let myself get lazy."
- "That was a good reminder to stay with my plan."
- "I guess I was forgetting to take care of myself."
- "There's something to learn from this."
- "Nobody said it would be easy."
- "I'll hang in there—there's a lot to be gained."
- "I'm in long-term training for a life-changing process."
- "I'm going to find my own ORDER and make it work."
- "I will be more mindful of my behaviors."
- "My OCD habit took years to develop—it'll take a while to unlearn."
- "I'm not a computer that can be instantaneously reprogrammed."

You may have already had a setback. What did you tell yourself? What did you learn from the setback? What made you vulnerable, and what did you do to become less vulnerable to future setbacks? Use the space below to jot down answers to these questions. You can look back at the list that you will develop later as a way to avoid setbacks.

Examine your setbacks, so that you can learn how you reverted to your old habits. Develop a plan that lets you:

1. Work on not overreacting to anxiety with obsessions and compulsive behaviors.

2. Keep yourself from mindlessly sleepwalking through the day.

3. Deal with each situation independently by observing yourself.

4. Keep yourself oriented in the here and now.

5. Focus on each task carefully, especially when you feel rushed.

Worrying is a slippery slope for obsessions. Perhaps you started worrying about your health. Then you do everything you can to find out the facts, to reduce your anxiety. You forgot that exposure to uncertainty is the antidote. To both neutralize the worrying and prevent a setback, be sure to apply exposure.

Whatever factors may have contributed to a setback, your plan is to learn from the experience, so that the setback can be worthwhile. Yes, worthwhile. Think of the setbacks as an opportunity to move ahead, rather than look back and lament.

Recognizing Mismanaged Anxiety Triggers of OCD

You are bound to experience anxiety every so often, because you are alive. Your success depends on how you manage it. To minimize your vulnerability to anxiety, expose yourself to various situations that triggered anxiety in the past, so that when they occur again you'll be prepared.

Many types of anxiety-producing stress that can trigger your OCD symptoms involve situations that are hard to prepare for in advance, such as arguments in your intimate relationships. Yet, there are things that you can do to minimize interpersonal stress. Challenging the relationship to grow by being open and flexible can minimize potential arguments in the future and break ground for the potential resolution of arguments. In this way you are also providing yourself with exposure.

On the other hand, when you hold on to checking behaviors (such as going to the doctor for every physical complaint), you increase the likelihood of relapse. Relapse prevention should include continual real-life exposure with response prevention to habituate yourself to situations you fear, such as letting chronic stomach concerns go unchecked. Expose yourself to the situation of an unlocked door if you're a checker. By making repeated exposures to the initial fear-provoking situation, you can form new associations to it. You can also develop positive self-talk to disprove your anxiety-provoking predictions of danger, such as it's not the end of the world if it really is unlocked.

As you develop your relapse prevention plan, keep in mind the context in which your OCD can get triggered again. If you keep practicing the ORDER method, the situations that trigger OCD will be lessened. Think of the context as filled with cues that trigger your anxious reactions. For example, the triggers for anxious reactions may occur within the context of stress at work or in your marriage. Another way to look at these potential triggers is that anxiety cues are like signals that alert you that something dangerous is coming. The problem is that many of them are false alarms. That's where exposure is so important. The greater the effort you make in the E and R parts of the ORDER method, the more your obsessions and compulsive behaviors will be reduced. Don't forget that exposure with response prevention is the most critical part of your long-term plan to tame your OCD.

What anxiety-provoking cues trigger your OCD symptoms? Use the worksheet below to note the cues that trigger your anxiety, the obsessions that then develop, your SUD score, the old OCD coping skills that you used, the skills you forgot to use, and your plan to modify your coping techniques. I filled in the first block as an example. By using this worksheet, you'll learn what triggered your old OCD pattern and what to do to prevent it.

CUES	OBSESSIONS	SUD SCORE 1–100	COMPULSIVE BEHAVIORS	WHAT I FORGOT TO DO	MY PLANNING
Husband leaving messes	What needs to be clean	85	Cleaning five times	Ask my husband to do his part	Be consistent in setting limits with my husband

Sometimes, the cues that trigger your OCD are unanticipated. They aren't as easily prepared for by exposure, and they take you by surprise. How can you plan for the unexpected? You can't know the future, but you can generally foresee situations that are anxiety provoking. This can be a tricky business, because you had a tendency in the past to overestimate danger. Here's what to do:

1. If you're still avoiding specific situations because you feel anxious about them, such as public restrooms, don't avoid them—expose yourself to them in a carefully planned way.

2. As anxiety-provoking situations come up, such as eating in a restaurant if that is a problem for you, use realistic measures to assess for true danger, including whether most people would find the situation dangerous or unbearable.

3. If you estimate that a situation is not danger-ous but merely anxiety provoking, begin graduated exposures.

4. Remember that exposure is your method of neutralizing OCD. As you identify the remain-ing cues, attack them with exposure.

Scott Converts an Anxiety Cue into an Opportunity

Scott's OCD symptoms centered on keeping his office impeccably ordered. In fact, he spent so much time arranging his office each day and putting "everything in its proper place" that he got behind in his work. His compulsion to arrange his office served as a way of procrastinating to avoid what he needed to do at work. Sometimes he spent so much time arranging his office that he got home late at night and his wife became angry with him. Only after his supervisor wrote him up did he come in for help. With the threat of job loss staring him in the face, he was very motivated. He learned how to apply the ORDER method relatively quickly. He discovered that one of the triggers for his obsessions and compulsive behaviors was that when he experienced stress at work in the form of no plans for a project, he tended to become obsessed with the order of things in his office. He then worked on shifting his priorities to creating a plan for the project. He applied the ORDER method to his efforts and managed to get his obsessions and compulsive behaviors to fade away.

It's critical to expose yourself consistently to those remaining anxiety-provoking cues in the response prevention part of the ORDER method, so that they no longer trigger OCD. By exposing yourself to these cues long after your anxiety has faded, you can con-tinue to habituate to them. This will engender a sense of durability and habituate your amygdala to them when you encounter these cues in the future. This will help deactivate your triggers, because you have made them innocuous. By continuing to expose yourself to them, you keep them converted.

When you examine the cues that trigger OCD, you give yourself a vantage point from which to recognize that many of them are associated with anxiety only in your mind. They are simply false alarms. Those cues can as easily be associated with innocuous experiences and with neutral or positive feelings. This conversion can only be accomplished by continual exposure to those cues.

Integrating Relapse Prevention Skills into Your ORDER

Throughout this workbook, you have challenged yourself to do things that didn't "feel right." You should congratulate yourself for these efforts. Your relapse prevention plan should involve integrating the parts of the ORDER method into long-term practice. Remind yourself of your accomplishments. Use them as examples of how to maintain your new perspective and to remind yourself that you are capable of meeting challenges that once seemed impossible.

No one technique of the ORDER method alone is sufficient for your long-term relapse prevention plan. A complete and durable plan includes all the techniques together. Relying on one or just a few techniques is like your car running on just a few pistons.

There are a number of things that you need to practice, so that your relapse prevention plan is integrated. Follow these guidelines:

- **Practice all the steps of the ORDER method.**
- **Practice good self-care habits; be sure to properly fuel your brain.**
- **Be sure to get enough sleep.**
- **Seek out the support of friends and family.**
- **Focus on the here and now to shift your attention away from anxiously worrying about the future.**
- **Expose yourself to situations that had triggered your OCD.**

Rating Your ORDER Skills

Staying with the ORDER method means practicing all the steps together on a regular basis. The more you practice them, the more they will become second nature to you. This is the power of neuroplasticity and what we mean by the ORDER-ABC. These steps will become the new habits that replace your old OCD habits.

SKILLS CHECKUP WORKSHEET

We want to determine which parts (of the full repertoire of practices) you have been weakest in developing, so that you can shore those up. Use the following worksheet to rate where you are strong and where you are weak. Rank them by assigning a number #1 for the strongest and so on. Also, write down your plan to improve that skill. This worksheet will help you practice remembering your relapse prevention skills.

SKILL	RANK	PLAN FOR IMPROVEMENT
Observing		
Reminding		
Doing		
Exposure		
Response Prevention		
Relaxation Skills		
Exercise		
Social Support		
Nutrition		

Note the skills you ranked the lowest. We want you to make those your strongest skills. Your first response might be: "Why not stay with the ones I like the best?" or possibly "What I've done already is good enough!"

You want to increase your durability as part of your relapse prevention plan. To promote durability, you'll need to strengthen your weak areas by practicing them more often and not rely solely on your strong suits. Consider this: You're only as strong as your weakest link. If you transform your weakest links into your strongest, your current strongest will be the weakest you ever are.

As you recall from chapter 10, healthy behaviors involve not only doing the things that help you relax but also things that add depth to your life. If you fall into a mode of always trying to relax, you'll relapse by developing anxiety sensitivity, which will trigger your OCD. You'll be so focused on reducing anxiety that any anxiety will feel like too much.

Strive for a flexible balance between excitement and relaxation, between your sympathetic and parasympathetic nervous systems. Your sympathetic nervous system gets you excited. It helps motivate you. Positive feelings activate the neurotransmitters dopamine, norepinephrine, and epinephrine (adrenaline).

Your parasympathetic nervous system helps calm you down. If you focus too much on one system and avoid the other, you can set yourself up for an imbalanced life and stir up anxiety, which triggers your OCD. You need both excitement and relaxation to keep your life varied, enjoyable, and balanced. Sound self-management, therefore, involves excitement as well as relaxation.

Don't forget that the way you perceive your symptoms or any given situation can stir up too much anxiety. Your relapse prevention plan should include striving to develop positive meaning for each experience in your life. Your automatic thoughts, assumptions, and core beliefs should have a positive spin, as detailed in chapter 5.

Prevention

Keep your long-term perspective. One of the most positive core beliefs you can embrace is the belief that you are always improving yourself and that you strive to enhance the quality and depth of your life.

Practice self-care. As you encounter stress or periods of anxiety in the face of difficult situations, practice good self-care. Self-soothing does not mean babying yourself. It simply means that you help yourself feel at ease during periods of stress by using all the relaxation skills that you've learned: diet, positive self-talk, imagery, and mindfulness.

Be flexible. As you face changes in your life and what you expected does not occur, face those situations as if you have shock absorbers. Don't forget that there are always bumps on the road.

Be resilient. Bouncing back from a rough time is one of the most important skills anyone can have. Resiliency is similar to flexibility but more of a major adjustment. Flexibility enables you to ride smoothly over the bumps on the road; resiliency gives you the ability to reconstitute yourself after a crisis.

Hang in there and resist responding. As you remember from practicing response prevention, compulsive behaviors are fool's gold. On the surface, they appear to be good ways to decrease anxiety, but they actually contribute to anxiety and OCD. Therefore, you want your relapse prevention plan to help you hang in there during exposures.

Stay with your exposure exercises. Consider them long-term treatments for OCD. You need a "maintenance dose" of exposure exercises over the long term to keep yourself habituated to the experiences that you once found anxiety provoking. Regular exposure is the way to stay "in condition."

Seek out social support. Social support, as noted earlier, is a critical part of your relapse prevention plan. Because you are human, key parts of your brain thrive on social contact. These systems comprise what has been called the "social brain." You'll need these systems fully activated. They were very much involved in your early bonding experiences with your parents. These regions of your brain, which include your orbital frontal cortex, are highly involved in the regulation of emotion. When you activate your social brain, you also activate the parts of your brain that control your emotions. So maintaining your social support system will help you keep a grip on your emotions.

Withdrawing from your social support system deactivates your social brain. Your orbital frontal cortex will then have less of a chance to dampen down your emotions. Even though you might not feel like being with people when you are anxious, social contact is nevertheless good for you. Think of it as "social medicine." Make sure that your relapse prevention plan includes a regular dose of social medicine.

Your relapse prevention plan should include many facets. Use the following worksheet to make sure that you adhere to all of them. In the date section of the worksheet, write down the date each week, to ensure that you stay on top of this. Use the blank spaces in the first column to write in specific parts of your unique plan. For example, if going to church or doing yoga is part of it, write it down. This will help you monitor all the parts of your plan, so that you don't leave anything out.

Relapse Prevention Monitoring Worksheet

	DATE	DATE	DATE	DATE	DATE	DATE	DATE	DATE	DATE
OBSERVING									
REMINDING									
DOING									
EXPOSURES									
RESPONSE PREVENTION									
RELAXATION SKILLS									
EXERCISE									
SOCIAL SUPPORT									
NUTRITION									

As you continue to work on your relapse prevention plan, remember that life itself is a challenge. And that's a good thing! Challenges make life interesting, exciting, and eventful.

Congratulations for having completed the exercises in this workbook! Your courage and continued adherence to the lessons learned in this book will keep OCD at bay. By practicing these exercises regularly, you will rewire your brain so that OCD is simply a bad habit that you left behind.

About the Authors

John B. Arden Ph.D., is the director of training for mental health for the Kaiser Permanente Medical Centers in Northern California. In this capacity, he oversees one of the largest mental health training programs in the world. He is the also the author of *The Heal Your Anxiety Workbook* and coauthor of *Conquering Post-Traumatic Stress Disorder* and *Brain-Based Therapy*.

Daniel DalCorso Psy.D., is subchief of Behavioral Medicine for Kaiser Permanente's Hayward-Fremont service area in Northern California. Obsessive-compulsive disorder has been a particular interest of his since his dissertation on the brain circuitry involved in OCD onset, maintenance, and treatment. He also co-founded and led the OCD treatment group while at Kaiser Permanente's Vallejo psychiatry department.